TIME
and
CHANCE

TIME
and
CHANCE

Marjorie Pegram

CHRISTIAN LITERATURE CRUSADE
Fort Washington, Pennsylvania 19034

ISBN 0-87508-594-6

Printed in the United States of America

Quotations from:
The King James Version of the Bible

To my precious Lord Jesus, who gave me this story.
To my beloved family.

I returned, and saw under the sun, that the race is not to the swift, nor the battle to the strong, neither yet bread to the wise, not yet riches to men of understanding, nor yet favour to men of skill; but time and chance happeneth to them all.

— Ecclesiastes 9:11

But let him that glorieth glory in this, that he understandeth and knoweth me, that I am the Lord. . . .

— Jeremiah 9:24a

CHAPTER 1

As the United 727 backed around for take-off, my glance out of the plane window lingered on Byrd Airport's waiting room where I knew Mother and Dad still watched. The glance became a gaze at the observation deck where my little brother Johnny would surely be watching my plane as it taxied down the runway. Did I see a wave from a certain twelve-year-old with blond hair? When I returned at summer's end, he would probably have grown two inches and never be a little guy again.

I'll miss him, I thought. How he envied me, going back to Europe, for a whole summer. The four of us had such a great time last summer on our first tour of Europe as a family, I reminisced as the plane gained speed, and excitement mounted doubly as I recalled a certain person, and — airborne! It never ceased to thrill me as the rough speeding wheels left the ground, and smooth flight toward the sky began.

I looked back down once more at the airport as the plane headed north on the 35-minute flight to D.C. So long, Mom and Dad. I'll miss you too. With his infectious smile, Dad had kissed me and said, "Behave yourself, Hon. The City of Light is full of those tigers, you know!" Mother had cried and couldn't do anything but hug and kiss me and give me her sad smile. She cried and fretted too much, and sometimes it irritated me, but this time I sort of broke a little too, inside. Guess I just hate partings.

As the stewardess took orders for drinks and the pilot gave his welcome over the intercom, I settled back, unbuckled my seat belt and began to think of the recent past. Graduation from Westhampton College of the University of Richmond over a month ago seemed an age with all the excitement of preparing for this long-awaited promise of Dad's. "Summer in Europe for your graduation present, since that seems to be your big desire. You can take some post-grad courses and even try to find some work to keep you busy and help me out some," he'd chuckled. Then more seriously, "And keep that tour director in line, and don't let him break your heart."

A thrill of joy possessed me as I remembered "that tour director," Ernst R. Neubauer, who had led our tour group last summer. My left thumb felt the cameo ring on my left hand as I gazed at it for the ten thousandth time. What exciting memories it brought to mind. His letters were all in one of my suitcases; the last letter and his cablegram in my purse. "Meet you 9:30 A.M. this side of Customs, Charles de Gaulle Airport, Paris, Tuesday, 17 June. Love, Ernst." I'd memorized it.

Tomorrow morning I'll see him at last! Almost a year since he kissed me goodbye at that same stunning airport, and said he'd try to fly to the States sometime during the year. But as it turned out, he couldn't, and all my friends were almost as disappointed as I — except for one. Frankie was glad, for I suspect he still rather dislikes the fellow, sight unseen. After all, he was supplanted in my affections, though I still like Frankie almost as much as ever, and we still date occasionally. I'm always available for a good time with a crowd. Quite in demand, though my heart is captured.

I thoughtfully sipped the Coke the stewardess had brought. Yes, my heart is captured, more recently by another Person. What a difference He has made in my life! Before I met the Lord Jesus Christ He was just a figure in history to me, not a real person at all. He'll never be just that to me again, for now I know that He is alive and working in the world today. All the uncertainties, doubts and conflicts which were getting to me, bearing me down, were turned over to Him, because I knew He could handle them and I couldn't. Yes, there are still problems which take time and effort to work out, but the absolutely great part is that they aren't mine any more. They're His responsibility, because He has promised in His Word, the Bible, that He'll take care of me! What glorious release and sheer joy His care and presence within me is and ever will be. He'll take care of this problem I face tomorrow, too, for He is Strength in the face of temptation.

I'd finished my Coke and dozed a bit when the pilot began to announce touch-down at Dulles International. Alert instantly, I wondered if Aunt Kate would be easy to find for our supper appointment before flight time at TWA at eight o'clock.

She was there at the Information desk after the process of landing, stepping from the plane onto that interesting reception-bus-room, and all the hustlebustle of late afternoon rush hour at D.C.'s Dulles. Seeing me coming, she waved, hurried toward me with arms outstretched and held me tightly a second. "Hi, Aunt Kate!"

"Melanie Alexander, let me look at you, my favorite beauty queen! More lovely and glowing than ever, and that's going some. Bless your heart. Let me take your

9

little bag. Have you checked your luggage through to Paris?"

"Yes, we took a big chance on their checking it through, so I just hope I don't have to wear these clothes all summer," I quipped, pushing my hair back.

"That's an adorable pants suit — matches your sparkling blue eyes. Let's find a little nook I know of and get a bite to eat. Can't waste a minute and risk your missing that eight o'clock flight!"

"No way, not *this* one!" I exclaimed, then gave her the family's greetings as we walked through the bustling crowds to an airport restaurant.

Seated and having given our orders, I glanced with admiration at Aunt Kate, dressed neatly as always in the latest fashion, her short, attractively styled ash-brown hair quite a contrast to my straight, waist-length light brown. I'd always loved my mother's younger sister, and especially so the last several months. She brusquely opened the conversation.

"First, how are Johnny and your parents taking your departure?"

"Johnny's wistful, Dad's his usual jovial, light-hearted self, and Mother cried. Before we reached the airport she said to give you her love. She was fearful she would break down — and she did."

"Poor Alyce, she always was teary, but I love her dearly. She's a precious sister, and I'm praying for her more than ever. She needs what you and I have found, that personal relationship with Jesus Christ, and I'm trusting she'll come through soon. Now, tell me all about yourself. Sorry, I just couldn't get off work to come down for your graduation, so we haven't talked for ages."

"Thank you again for the card and gift, Aunt Kate. I've been so swamped with preparations that my phone call thanks had to suffice."

"Don't mention it, but you'd better write me from Paris — that's an order, dear! I'm still planning a short visit over, but haven't firmed up plans yet. I'll let you know details later." She's quite a procrastinator, I recalled, but though brusque and breezy, very efficient.

"I hope you can come while I'm there. You are going with Ernst's agency, aren't you?"

"Of course, and don't worry, I'll see that I hit Paris first and last, if possible. I doubt I'll go on an organized tour, but if I do, you know how unlikely it is that I'd get him as director."

"Wouldn't it be neat if you could? I'd be very jealous of you, going off with him while I had to stay behind in Paris," I said, then grew serious. "Aunt Kate, there's something I've never told you. Oh, I told a couple of my close friends, but certainly not Mother and not even Dad. Frankly, I don't know whether he'd have croaked or guffawed."

She was all sympathetic attention, but at that moment the waitress came with our orders, so I waited, then a bit self-consciously asked, "Would you — pray?"

"Certainly, dear," and she asked the blessing, a privilege we'd agreed to exercise even when eating in public.

I had to have it out before I could eat, so I dove in. "Last summer, after we got to Paris, you may remember my telling you that Ernst, some of the other kids and I spent the afternoon and evening together — our last day before flying back home. Well, the others finally left us together and, even though we'd only been fairly well acquainted a few days, Ernst gave me a sort of proposal. He said he could arrange for me a free tour of Europe any time, if I would pose as his wife. Well, he painted a beautiful picture, when my appetite was already whetted

11

with all the fabulous things we'd seen, and frankly, I was really tempted —"

Aunt Kate reached out and put her hand gently on mine. "The old dishonorable proposal, old as time, but I don't blame you. What a temptation it must have been."

"I was pretty much in love at that point, and just a few days earlier at the cameo factory on our way to Tivoli Gardens in Rome with the tour group, he'd given me this ring just as a little gift, as he put it, a token of his affection. I think, as tired as I was, I could easily have turned around and gone with him on his very next tour. I was no innocent kitten either, I'm ashamed to say, and I knew the score, though we hadn't . . . . "

She nodded in understanding and apparent relief.

"We'd hit the bars and of course he could hold his much better, and I guess I was a bit fuzzy and on top of creation, but he was dead serious with all the details worked out. Well, I knew I'd have to check with Dad and Mother, but we were to leave early next morning, and it was pretty wee hours when we returned to the hotel. Of course I'd have to give Dad some heavy persuasion, that it would all be a gift from Ernst, imply separate rooms and so on — but it would have to be done right then, no waiting till morning."

I sipped my Coke and took a bite as she nodded. "Yes, of course."

"So after Ernst left me, I tapped on their door till Dad came and let me in. Mother was sound asleep and of course Johnny was in another room. To keep it short, he either saw through it or was just too sleepy to compute details, but he strongly advised me to come back as planned and think it over after we all got home. If I still wanted to go with Ernst later in the summer or this next year, maybe it could be arranged. Well, frankly, I nearly threw a fit, for I really wanted to stay. You know how determined I am when I want to do something."

"Yes, I'd say that was always one of your, ah, strong points, or should I say, foibles?" She winked, and I had to agree.

"Mostly my foibles. Do you know, he took me to my room, sat me down and reasoned with me till I *very* unhappily submitted, then left me to lie awake for hours, after calling Ernst to tell him the decision. All the ifs and possible arrangements, then disappointment and frustration kept dragging through my brain till I finally fell asleep about dawn. Well, I slept through breakfast and didn't wake up till Mother came in to help me get ready and onto that awful local bus to the airport. Of course I couldn't speak to Ernst at the hotel with all the confusion of the last morning, everyone saying good-bye and so on. Then he met us at the airport, arranged our departure and told everyone good-bye, and finally he and I sadly parted with a kiss."

She was mercifully silent for a few seconds. "I know what a rough time you must have had, Mel. Your dad surely must have seen through it right away. My brother-in-law is no fool." She paused. "Evidently you decided not to go back after you got home, but you must have made a dozen decisions back and forth all year, at least till lately."

"Yes. Of course, there was Frankie to square with, for we had an understanding, almost an engagement. But he wasn't ever quite the same to me after Ernst. Frankie was pretty deeply hurt, but I couldn't help it. I still definitely hoped to go back this summer, one way or another — to work or go to school . . . or travel with Ernst. It sure was rough on me for months, battling with conscience, desire, worry, anticipation. You know some of the family problems on top of everything else in my senior year, including my Art History thesis — no big deal except it was like the proverbial straw. Some of my friends were so helpful, especially a couple of Christians who hadn't the foggiest idea what was bothering me most. We have a neat group of committed Christians at U.R. in the Inter-Varsity Christian Fellowship, Aunt Kate, as I found out later. Between you and them, I finally came through the fog and found the Way, as you know. Actually, they were the final instruments God used, along with you and your prayers before that."

Aunt Kate said, "Yes, after I met Jesus, I really prayed hard for you, Mel. Then your granddad's death in the winter hit your mother and me pretty hard, especially her, for she was very dependent on him. I had Christ to comfort me, and I know Dad was a Christian; but Alyce admittedly isn't close enough to Him, so she's suffered more over it."

"You're right. It was hard on us all. I wish I were as sure that my dad's a Christian as you were about yours — Granddad," I sighed. "But you know, Aunt Kate, this was another of my worries. Would I end up being melancholy like Mother? That's a miserable thing to admit, and of course it's no longer any concern, because I love her so much more. You know my burden for her and Dad, but it bothered me a lot, and made me feel guilty too. I'm so glad He took all those hang-ups away."

"Bless you, I know how it is, for I had lots of them too before He became my Savior and Lord, and took them off my shoulders. You were too young to know much about what a mess my life was. What a difference knowing Him makes! But Mel, of course you realize you're going into the fire now. It won't be easy. . . ."

"Oh, I know it! I *wrote* Ernst about my conversion, and at first he didn't seem to know what to say except 'that's interesting.' But I had no intention of letting it drop, so next letter I said a little more. He answered with a question or two, but in the last letter he admitted he'd thought a lot about the philosophy of death and freedom, etc., and said maybe we could discuss it sometime. No 'maybe' about it, Aunt Kate! The Lord means so much to me that I have to share Him with Ernst — I'm *determined* to!"

"Good for you, Mel, you always did have a lot of courage and true grit. When you set your mind to something, you always go at it full force."

"Well, guess you're right on. He did say the proposal still stands, but of course that's out for me now. It's ominous, and I'm rather nervous. I love him, Aunt Kate, but I know he may not be the one for me now, unless he comes to faith in Jesus."

"Yes. 'Be ye not unequally yoked...'" she quoted. "Not that marriage has been mentioned," and I nodded in agreement. "You know I'll be praying night and day for him, and you, dear, that the old tempter doesn't overcome, and for your witness to him."

"I know you will, and so will I. Let's form a prayer pact, for, what is that promise in Matthew? . . . 'If two of you shall agree on earth as touching anything that they shall ask . . .'"

"'. . . it shall be done for them of my Father which is in Heaven,' Matthew 18:19," she quoted with me, for we had both memorized it. "Also don't forget I John 5:14 and 15."

"Right. That prayer pact goes for Mother and Dad too, Aunt Kate."

"It's a deal, Melanie. I'll be with you all the way." We talked of other matters, soon finished eating, then she glanced at her watch. "Don't know where the time has gone, but it's getting on towards seven o'clock, and we'd better get back."

"Yes. This has been wonderful, Aunt Kate. I'm so grateful for you, and for all you mean to me."

"You're pretty special to me too, sweetheart."

CHAPTER 2

We'd said our good-byes and I'd gone through the boarding process and now sat waiting for one more door to open for admittance to the 747 jet. More and more people came to sit or stand near the entrance, filling the room. I watched with almost the excitement I'd felt a year ago as we waited to board. Johnny had been quite roguish and boy-like, I reminisced with a tiny smile. I was not the seasoned traveler by any means, yet with a tinge of amusement I sensed the subdued excitement of those around me.

Reflecting on the advice Aunt Kate had given me before we parted with a short prayer, I recalled her suggestion that I think and pray about writing Mother and Dad the whole truth about Ernst's proposal. My reaction had been negative until she emphasized the value of complete honesty with them, even if they did perhaps know the situation. She suggested that if trouble of any kind arose, it would be better had I been honest early in the game, if not at first. After a few seconds' thought I could see her point, though it wouldn't be easy to confess now.

Then she'd told me, "Remember, Melanie, God has a definite purpose for your life, right now as you go to France, and don't forget that He's not finished working with and in you. So if you make a mistake, remember that and don't get discouraged. Forgiveness is only a confession away, and He loves us, even when we make mistakes."

I was sure she really knew of what she spoke, for she had suffered a lot before finally giving in and submitting to Jesus Christ, and I had a feeling that her counsel might be needed more than once.

At last a stewardess opened the door, and as we were ushered into the plane I once again marveled at the enormity of its interior, an auditorium on invisible wheels. Fortunate to get a seat next to a window, I settled my belongings and self for the night's journey. A couple sat down beside me, so engrossed in each other that I didn't attempt much conversation.

After some short delays, the huge jet was soon taxiing and then — airborne for our transatlantic flight at last! Squeezing my eyes tightly shut for a second, I thought with a thrill, only a few more hours till I see him! My genial Austrian friend from Vienna who, like our illustrious Secretary of State, was still unable to pronounce the *w*, and the *th* was almost a *d*. I yearned to hear his thick accent again.

With his fluency in four languages and familiarity with a fifth, he had much encouraged my study of French, my second major at Westhampton along with Art History. The test of my linguistic ability was to come as I would take up residence in Paris and try to perfect my pronunciation at the Alliance Française of the University of Paris. Almost two weeks of freedom till my studies there began. Paris, avec Ernst! Well, some of it with him, as he would probably leave for a tour before my course began. Only seven more hours to squeeze in a night's sleep, with both dinner and breakfast on the plane. Nine-thirty A.M. Paris time would be a sleepy four-thirty A.M. for me, but it certainly wouldn't be the first night I'd had so few hours' sleep.

The couple next to me carried on such a constant conversation interspersed with kisses that I grew more anxious than ever to see Ernst. Taking his last letter from my purse, I reread it, thrilling again to its contents, though with a feeling of wariness because of the task I'd set myself to do when we would meet again.

Dearest Melanie,

Yours received, mein Mädchen — danke. Your excited anticipation increases mine. Only wait till you're here with me — hurry the time . . . .

It's been tight here too. Papers, theses, exams, as you call them, endless details to see to, on top of tour preparations, lining up schedules, finances, correspondence ad nauseum. Things are going as planned, however, and I will meet your plane at Charles de Gaulle when you arrive on Tuesday, 17 June, after you get through Customs, as I told you before.

This experience you described to me, of, as you called it, "submitting your life to Jesus Christ the Lord," still rather puzzles me. As I mentioned before, I have for a long time searched for self-identity, and what could be the real meaning of our lives, if you know what I mean. Yes, of course I know Jesus lived in what became the first century, but I can't say that he claimed to be God, or that he lives in some sort of "spiritual body." What is this "spiritual body"? It makes no sense to me. You asked what I think of death, etc. I have thought quite a lot about the philosophy of death and freedom, which I feel is supreme, because I am nihilistic. This gets too involved on paper. Maybe we can discuss it sometime.

My arms await you, ma chérie, and I anticipate showing you more of Europe. The offer still stands, you know.

Au revoir, mon amour,

Ernst

Oh, Father, I begged my Lord, *please help me to know how to share You with Ernst.* Knowing him as I do and from his letters, I thought, my witness to him *must* be verbal as well as his just seeing the change in my life — what I am now. I'm sure he's the kind of person who needs to have ideas communicated — to rap with. His intelligence demands a verbal exchange of beliefs. *Fill me with Your Spirit, Lord, that I may exhibit Your love, reveal Your joy and peace, and Your patience!*

As I prayed, I felt the strong urge to read a certain passage of Scripture. Taking my little pocket-size Bible from my purse, I opened it to Ezekiel 3:18, 19, reading, "When I say unto the wicked, Thou shalt surely die; and thou givest him not warning, nor speakest to warn the wicked from his wicked way, to save his life; the same wicked man shall die in his iniquity; but his blood will I require at thine hand. Yet if thou warn the wicked, and he turn not from his wickedness, nor from his wicked way, he shall die in his iniquity; but thou hast delivered thy soul." The import of the words burned into my soul. Next to the passage I had jotted another reference, James 5:20, to which I turned and read, "Let him know, that he which converteth the sinner from the error of his way shall save a soul from death, and shall hide a multitude of sins." What a goal was mine!

It was then as though the Lord whispered in my spirit, "This is the way, walk ye in it. Trust Me, and I will prepare the way before you." I sensed the presence of Jesus very near to me.

Later, after a delicious foretaste of French cookery for our late dinner, I decided to forego the proffered film choices and try to get to sleep, or as we sometimes reversed our Shakespeare, "to dream, perchance to sleep."

What seemed a minute later, the stewardess was shaking me awake with a question, "Would you like some orange juice?"

"Mm . . . ." I murmured sleepily. "Hm?"

She patiently repeated her question and explained, "We're approaching the west coast of France. Breakfast will soon be served. It's seven-fifteen A.M., Paris time."

"Oh! Yes, thank you." I soon roused myself, smoothed back my untidy hair and sipped some juice to get more awake. The couple next to me was curled up in each other's arms, sound asleep, and a boy was at one of the windows pushing aside the black-out curtains to reveal the brilliantly shining sun. I did the same, recalling how Johnny and I had pushed them aside almost a year ago as we flew across southwestern England on our way to London. How thrilling it had been to be flying over the land of all the literary greats of the past! *Oh Father, good morning,* I breathed, *and thank You for a safe flight so far, and for the rest, for I trust You for it all.*

Even the continental breakfast was too much at two-forty A.M. by my stomach, so I sipped some coffee to stay awake. Some time later the pilot spoke over the intercom that we were approaching the environs of Paris, were on time, and would touch down about eight-forty A.M. at Charles de Gaulle Airport. We had gone above and through thick snowy clouds, but the weather in Paris was reportedly sunny and warm. As superb as it was that unforgettable day last August? I asked myself with a thrill of excitement as I sat glued to my window staring down at the lovely city and noting some of its familiar landmarks. How Eiffel towered the lower we came, beckoning to me, as did the quiet Seine meandering through her seductive surroundings.

We slowly filed out of the plane after a smooth landing, into the "satellite" moving passageway leading to the central arrival hall. Quivering with anticipation, I prayed I'd find my luggage on the conveyor belt, and that our first day together again would go especially well. Would he be different from the picture he'd sent me and from my much faded memory of his face?

It seemed eternity watching the conveyor, on the elliptical-shaped carousel bringing everyone's luggage but mine, which finally appeared. Then came another long wait in one of the lines to go through Customs. Finally I was free, and gazed around the sea of faces in the huge area when I heard a voice almost next to me, with a certain Austrian flavor.

"Looking for someone, young lady?"

"Ernst?" I turned and searched his face. "Ernst!"

He held out his arms to me and I went straight into them.

"Melanie," he murmured, his face buried in my hair. I surrendered to the warm gentleness of his embrace, and our lips met in joy.

"Ma belle," he said as he looked down into my eyes and softly touched my hair. "You are even lovelier than before."

"Oh Ernst! Thank you. We're together again, and it's all so perfect!" Oblivious to the crowds around us, I couldn't take my eyes from his face — his small twinkling brown eyes full of understanding, expressive lips closed in a smile, slightly rugged tanned skin, sideburns and black shock of hair across his forehead, just the right length around his ears and brushed toward the back of his neck. Tall and slim, he wore a plaid knit jacket and solid tan trousers. "Perfect," I repeated, feeling radiant.

"Do you know, I shaved my beard for you," he chuckled.

"Really? That's right, you did mention growing a beard. Why did you shave it? Did you think I'd object?"

"No, I thought you might not recognize me," he teased. "I grew it after I sent you my picture."

"Wouldn't it have been ghastly if I hadn't recognized you!" I giggled impishly. "Wonder what you looked like."

"A bearded man," drily. "I'll show you a picture later. Now we must take care of you, ma chérie. Did all your luggage arrive?"

"Yes, it's all here, thank the Lord."

"I have booked you for as long as you need to stay at a pension in southeast Paris, quite close to a metro stop. My room is next to yours. It costs considerably less than a hotel, as you requested. Let's see to your luggage and get on our way."

We went by taxi, "in dubious style, just this once" as Ernst said, and I snuggled against him under his arm as we caught up on our recent past.

"How long do we have together, and when is your next tour?"

"I just finished my first yesterday and my next begins from here next Monday. I managed to fix it to have more time between tours than usual. At least for a few days before your classes begin, you could go along, my dear?"

"Ernst —" I began, but he must have seen my slight frown, for he stopped me.

"No, no, we'll talk about it later. Not now, mein Mädchen. Now, you must just look at our city and enjoy her sights."

"How did you do at Zürich — the university — since you wrote?" I asked, somewhat relieved about postponing serious discussion.

"My studies in architecture are progressing. After so many years a 'perpetual college student,' I have at last settled down to a specialty, and my dad and mother are very happy."

"How are your two sisters?"

"Oh, quite the young ladies. Reni is seventeen now, Anna fifteen. They're beginning to tease me about being twenty-five and never getting married." I noticed his slight frown which as quickly disappeared, along with a change of subject, inquiries of my parents and Johnny. Then he took out his wallet and showed me pictures of his sisters and himself with his beard. We both agreed he looked better shaved.

"See, we are almost here. This pension is one we have used on some of our tours, and the concierge and clerk are friends of mine. You'll like Henri, Melanie. He's young, and you can practice your French on him, because he doesn't speak English."

Inside the lobby at the desk, Ernst introduced me to the desk clerk, Henri Bonnard, quite a handsome blond, hazel-eyed fellow who looked mid-twentyish. We conversed briefly in French. I settled my bill, then we took my luggage up to my room.

"This is — very adequate, Ernst," I said as we entered and I glanced around, for it was only temporary until I could move into school quarters, and I had asked him to find something less than first quality. A lovely fragrance filled the room, and I saw a huge bouquet of red roses on the table in front of floor-length-draped, sun-lit high windows.

"Oh, look, Ernst!" I walked over and read the card, which said, "Welcome to the City of Light, ma chère Melanie. Je t'aime. Ernst."

"Oh darling! Thank you so much. You know my favorite. They're beautiful, so fragrant, and — I love you!"

He took me into his arms murmuring, "Ich liebe dich." His lips sought and found mine, and my heart pounded. Together at last! With a deep sigh, he held my shoulders and said a mite shakily, "Perhaps you'd like to settle in a bit, and I'll be in my room. Then we'll get something to eat."

"Yes, that sounds good. I remember you never eat breakfast, and you must be hungry."

"A little. You do remember my habits."

We decided to eat in the pension dining room, and I relished every mouthful of the tempting omelet with ham cooked as only the French can, and café au lait. When I bowed my head first for a silent thanks, I felt his eyes on me, but he offered no comment.

"Are you too tired to stroll some?" he asked as we left the dining room.

"I'm not a bit tired. It'll hit me later, but especially tomorrow. Let me do some unpacking and freshening up, then you know I'd love to go downtown and walk along the Seine this afternoon — could we? — by the river and around the Left Bank where we walked a year ago?"

"Of course! As your heart desires, meine Lieber. I'll talk with Henri and meet you here. Take your time. We have plenty of it."

I wrote down a short promised message of safe arrival to my parents, which he said he would send by cable while I freshened up.

CHAPTER 3

Later, on the way to the metro stop, we passed an open air sidewalk market two blocks long, filled with all kinds of fragrant flowers in season, fruits and vegetables. We bought some fruit for a snack, and the salesman said with a broad smile, "Des fleurs pour la belle demoiselle?"

Ernst bought a rose and gaily laced it into my hair. "For you a rose."

"Merci, mon chéri." As we walked on, I pushed my hair back and exclaimed, "Oh, it's so super to be in Paris again — with you!"

He squeezed my hand and said, "A lovely day ordered for a very pretty girl."

We rode the metro to the Place St.-Michel station and ascended the steps to behold across the narrow Seine the twin towers of the majestic Notre Dame Cathedral spreading her benediction over all her surroundings. Halfway across the Pont St.-Michel, we stopped and gazed around at many famous landmarks, small boats and bridges, each of which he identified for me just as he had done a year ago. I took a few pictures with my small camera. Then we strolled hand in hand down some steps to the lowest walkway along the river. How I loved it there. This was the place I chose to tell him the most precious experience of my life, but it was hard to begin, even after a silent prayer for wisdom. My reckless determination won out, however, and I began.

"Ernst, I can paint fair pictures with my hands, and one day soon I'll bring my paints down here and give it a try, but I'm not much with words. . . ."

"You write quite interesting letters."

"Well—thanks—but . . . ." Swallowing hard, I pushed on with determination. "I want to tell you more about my experience of the Lord Jesus Christ, and His reality in my life, since I came to know Him two and a half months ago." I paused, and he nodded with an indulgent smile. "Ernst, I—think I wrote you that I never thought of Him except as some long past figure of history, you know, and I'd be amused at people who made such a big fuss over all the much-touted events of His life and death. Christmas and Easter were just big celebrations and new clothes to me. But this past year, suddenly, everything converged on me like . . . like spokes on the wheel of history, and I was just turning round and round getting nowhere, until I found the hub and became one with it. A silly illustration . . . ."

"Maybe you just 'grew up' this year. You've had a hard one."

"Yes, maybe, but it's much more than that. I found the Reason for life that I never could find before. Who are we, why are we here, what's it all about, why do we — as Moses wrote —'spend our years as a tale that is told' ? I finally met, face to face, the Eternal Answer, the Son of God, the One who paid the penalty on the cross for every sin of which we're all guilty! He's alive, Ernst, He really did arise. He's a real Person. And we can know Him in an actual, personal relationship. He's not only in Heaven, but here in spirit form, the Holy Spirit, and active in the world today!"

"Oh? You think this 'person' is 'active' in the world? Is he active in Vietnam, Cambodia, and the Middle East with all the suffering hordes of poor hovel-dwellers escaping from liberation? Active in China and Russia and her ... how do you say, satellites? It looks to me more like the Marxists have pretty well silenced and conquered Him. Is He active in your government which declines to honor its former commitments as it covers up scandals? In your people? And in mine, who are more concerned for the high cost of living than for helping to alleviate suffering of the less fortunate?"

These so true accusations would have overwhelmed me had I not questioned them myself and found at least fair answers. I sat down on the low stone embankment at the river's edge. "Yes, Ernst, He is active in ways invisible to many. He has chosen and bought with His very life, sacrificed on a cross of death, certain people in the world, and He is working out His purposes in and through them — us. God, through the Holy Spirit, is in the process of remaking His children into beings like His Son. 'Conforming us to the image of His Son,' as the Apostle Paul said it in his letter to the Romans."

A sardonic smile crossed his face as he sat down beside me. "You seem very certain of being among the few 'chosen.' You are very close to being an angel, but I didn't count on your being *that* close!" The smile turned sweeter, and with a sinking feeling I realized it was saccharine, and lashed out.

"Come off it, Ernst. I didn't count on your sarcasm, either. I make no claim to be either angelic or 'good,' though I do try to please my Lord. I fight sin every day, and too often lose. Then Satan laughs when he gets the victory."

"Ach, come now," he said roguishly. "Don't tell me

you actually believe in that creature with the red suit, horns and long tail!"

"Good grief, Ernst. Don't be ridiculous." He seemed to be stringing me along with his humor, and, a bit piqued, I said, "He doesn't have to look like that to exist. He comes in many guises — 'angels' even, sometimes, it says in Scripture. Whom do you think the Satan worshipers you read about worship?"

"Their imagination, probably. The human psyche is capable of incredible things." Oh no, you're wrong, I thought. "I'm afraid, Melanie, I can't get excited over religion. I've heard it all before, from years ago. Not that my family was ever religious; though, come to think of it, my grandmother was a church person. Catholicism today in Austria is dead, and that's about all I have. It's a mockery."

I caught the acrid flavor in his voice and eyes, and full of real compassion, my heart cried out, It isn't true, Ernst! There are missionaries of the Cross ministering in Austria and other European countries, in the Mid-East and all over the world. If only you knew. If only you knew Him! *Open his eyes, Lord,* I prayed.

He continued in a bitter tone, "The priests hold their liquor better than I do, and their hypocrisy you wouldn't believe. In fact, I'm disillusioned about not only clergy but religious people in general."

"There's far more hypocrisy in the world than there is in the church," I said, "though I agree the church as a whole has become too worldly. As my pastor, Rev. Fesmire, recently said in a sermon, he'd rather spend a few years with the hypocrites in the church than spend eternity with them in Hell." I paused thoughtfully, again breathing a prayer for God's wisdom. "What you've seen and heard may be a mockery, Ernst, but it's not 'religion' or 'the church' that's the important thing. The vital fact is that God in Christ is bringing many in the world to Himself, slowly, it seems, yes. We're all sinners, Ernst, everyone in the world has broken God's laws, failed to be what He wants us to be, come short of His glory, not only by what we've done, but what we've left undone." With quaking heart, I took my little Bible from my shoulder bag. "Will you please let me show you three or four verses in the book of Romans?"

I heard his faint sigh, but went ahead with shaky courage as I read from the third chapter, " ' . . . there is none that doeth good . . . all have sinned. . . .' Then in the sixth, 'For the wages of sin is death. . . .' But look, Ernst, here in the fifth chapter, verse eight, 'But God commendeth his love toward us, in that, while we were yet sinners, Christ died for us.' And — "

He interrupted me coldly, "Don't show me any more, and don't bother quoting Scripture to me, Melanie. I'm sure you probably know a lot about it." The sarcasm in his words cut pretty deep, but apparently to soften the cruel impact of his last statement, he conceded, "Maybe later. Tomorrow, more, all right?"

Tomorrow, I thought with fragile hope and dismal disappointment, but I smiled a bit sadly, and said, "Sure. Let's go on and walk some more." I knew I'd antagonized him and blown it, but I took his hand as we walked on silently toward the Ile St.-Louis and the end of the walkway. *Thank You, Lord, for helping me, anyway,* I prayed, trying hard to obey the "Rejoice always."

A couple with arms entwining each other met us walking the opposite way, and we smiled. Ernst glanced back at them a few seconds later and chuckled.

"Look behind us." They were deeply in embrace, kissing. He stopped me and took me in his arms too, saying "Let's be copycats, you beautiful zealot, you!"

I took his kiss self-consciously, wondering who else

was enjoying our abandon from the street above, or behind us, and gave him a gentle push. He said playfully, "In Paris, anything goes, ma chérie."

"Only in Paris would I ever do it," I said shamelessly, then rebuked myself with a mental punch. "No, I'm sorry. Location has no bearing on right or wrong."

"Said the parrot."

"You're full of sarcasm today! Are you always like that?"

"Often, when provoked, but I don't call that sarcasm, only joshing," he grinned, then said, "At least, meine Lieber, I'm not an atheist. You should be grateful for that."

"Oh, I am, and I praise the Lord for that. He loves you too, Ernst, enough to die on a cross for you."

As though he hadn't heard, he continued, "All this beauty had to have a beginning, at least a beginning. That I'll concede. And I feel a belief in God is enough." He gazed at the brilliantly blue Paris sky, the blooming flowers and verdant trees, the passenger boat gliding by on the Seine, then down at me, squeezing my shoulders with his arm. "Do you remember the first time I kissed you?"

"Could I ever forget, chéri? In Florence, almost a year ago, on my twenty-first birthday, when you set up a birthday celebration after dinner for our whole tour group, all for me. You came over and shook my hand, wished me happiness, then bent down and kissed me! That's when I fell in love with you. Before that, you were only a rather-better-than-ordinary tour director."

He chuckled impishly, "On almost every tour there's at least one to do it for. Of course, I don't give a kiss when the husband is there. Too risky!"

We laughed as we ascended the steps to the street full of speeding cars (how they raced in Paris!), lingered at the displays of the artists on every block, watched them sketch or paint, and bought a couple of small prints and post cards. As we had a year ago, we walked over to the Boulevard St.-Germain, and turned west again through the Latin Quarter toward the university, seeing the imposing tower of the Panthéon above the other buildings.

"Guess in a couple of weeks this'll be as familiar as home to me," I said, and he showed me around the university, then on down the Boulevard Raspail to the Alliance Française, where I would register, have classes, and live.

After strolling through the elegant Luxembourg Gardens and the Palais, we dined at the Bistro Petit Montmorency. When we'd finished, he said, "You must be getting tired, and I suggest we go back and you get to bed early tonight, and sleep late tomorrow. I must take care of some details for my next tour in the morning. You'll join me then for lunch and afterward?"

"Yes, sure will, thank you, and I am a bit tired. I want you to take me on the grand tour, as you offered, while we're together and have the chance."

"We'll have lunch in la Tour Eiffel and begin from there. And I suggest for your benefit we begin to speak in French tomorrow, n'est-ce pas?"

"Tres bonne idée, mon chéri."

When we got to my door at the pension, it was well past dark, and I felt a warm bath and the bed a welcome duo and said as much. "It's been a big day."

"When you finish and rest a bit, may I come back for a few minutes, to talk some more?"

"Yes, for a while, Ernst. Three soft knocks, okay?"

He nodded and with a light kiss left me.

While I drew my bath water, I giggled as I noticed again the inevitable French bidet that Ernst had explained and joked about on the loud speaker of the motor coach to the group last summer on our entering France. I had tried one but scorned it now.

After my bath, I lay on the bed a few moments, but the intense excitement of his imminent coming made me restless, so I sat at the little table and started the letter to Mother and Dad that Aunt Kate had suggested. I hadn't written much when three soft knocks sent me to unlock the door, which he closed when he entered.

"You look more rested and comfortable, and smell so good," he said.

"Most of the scent is your bouquet, Ernst. It's so lovely, and I like my room too, in the evening. Do sit down."

He declined, glanced at the table and said, "I'm glad you're pleased. I see you've already begun a letter. How admirable."

"There's lots to tell Mother and Dad."

He looked down in my eyes, drew me to him and held me close, then whispered softly in my ear, "I want you, Melanie. Very much. Tonight."

Apprehension filled me and a certain inner voice said, Be careful. It was painfully familiar territory. If we love each other, what harm? Prove our love. Same words, same meaning. Gently, firmly I put him off. How, I don't know, for I wanted him too, and our love would have made it all so easy. Some force stronger than I, within and around me, kept me from falling. Strangely enough, he understood, or at least acquiesced, and relieving an awkward silence, he told me of his projected tour.

"It'll be similar to the tour you had last year, only it begins where yours ended, and ends in London. First we go to Switzerland, then to Italy." Again he looked straight into my eyes as he mentioned the cities that held so many of our little memories: Lucerne, Rome, Florence, Venice. . . . "Remember how you threw your coins into Trevi Fountain? And Tivoli...." He looked at the ring he'd given me on the way there, touching it gently. "You'll go along, Melanie?"

Temptation, turmoil tore at my being. Total fatigue at the end of such a superb day caused my head to spin.

"Oh, Ernst, we'll talk about it tomorrow. But I'm afraid I — I mustn't," I pushed back my hair from my face wearily.

"Of course, chérie. You're very tired, and I'll leave now. Until noon tomorrow, bonne nuit." His kiss was soft, so sweet, and when he closed the door I locked it silently, sadly.

CHAPTER 4

Weakly I sank to my knees by the bed, closed my eyes and stayed there a long time. Dozens of pictures, mostly of Ernst's face in all its various expressions, crossed my mind, and I began to pray.

"Father, precious Lord Jesus, thank You for this perfect day. . . . For a safe journey, for Ernst, for this room, for all we did together, for his love, his gentleness, his understanding . . ." My eyes misted as I went on, " . . . for the few words I could tell him of You and Your loving plan, and mostly for the strength You gave me tonight, Lord. You know I wanted him. I love him so much. You know my weakness, and You gave me Your strength. Thank You, Jesus. You were tempted too, so You knew how to help me, and You did. Praise You, Jesus. Please open his eyes to Yourself and Your truth, Father. Use me in any way You can. Be my wisdom and strength for tomorrow, precious Lord. Show me what I can say to him."

I reached for my Bible I'd put on the bedside table and read some of the Psalms which had become dear to me, and some New Testament passages on God's plan of salvation, until I got so sleepy even on my knees that I had to give up and climb into bed where I soon knew no more.

Drowsily I opened one eye to discover the time on my travel clock. Almost 10 A.M.! The sounds of the city traffic below had for some time penetrated my consciousness, but now I roused myself. A delicious languor possessed me as my thoughts filled with yesterday's events, a thrill of joy as I recalled Ernst's kisses. The room was gloomy with no sunlight at the windows, a cloudy day that boded ill for sightseeing.

Something was nagging at my brain. It was something Ernst had said yesterday. What was it he'd said about hovel-dwellers in Vietnam escaping from "liberation"? And the Marxists having pretty well silenced and conquered God? "Liberation." The familiar word played to a different tune in the States. . . . Surely not Marxist sympathies? Apprehension filled me as I realized how little I really knew about him. On the tour last year, I recalled he'd run into a certain fellow in a few of the cities we visited, to whom he would talk privately. One time as I stood nearby I had heard snatches of what was surely German. One evening the group went to a live show and he left after getting us in. Afterwards the two were together when we boarded the bus to return to our hotel. How silly, I rebuked myself; surely just a friend, meeting by coincidence or plan.

Then my thoughts took another track. This decision he wanted me to make returned to mind. I knew very well I had no business even considering it, yet it was so tempting. To how many others had he made the same proposal? Who, for instance, was that chic local guide in London last year who had come to our hotel lobby when we all first arrived, asking breezily where her husband the tour director was? I got that tidbit by rumor from some of the girls who'd heard her and laughed over the incident, and I'd forgotten it till now. Well, he'd certainly never pretended to be a saint. . . . Wonder why he'd really shaved his beard? Surely not merely so I'd recognize him, as he'd said.

Ridiculous turn my thoughts were taking. Must be the weather, I persuaded myself as I got up and looked out the open window, hoping it wouldn't rain. After reading some in my Bible and praying, I busied myself with details and then sat down to continue the letter to Mother and Dad, but had to stop before getting to the hard part, because it was getting near noon. Determined to do it the very next chance I had, I began a paragraph with, "There's a confession I need to make to you." That would make it easier when the time came.

Just as I finished getting ready, a minute or two after twelve, three knocks sounded and I greeted Ernst at the door. He looked good in an open neck sport shirt and a raincoat held over his shoulder with his index finger, a familiar stance I recalled from last year.

He greeted me in French, suggested the probable need for my raincoat too, and we were soon off. The concierge was in Henri's place at the desk in the lobby, and Ernst introduced me to her. Later he expained when I asked about Henri, "He's on duty nights till about mid-morning or something like that."

Our lunch of steak-Bordeaux in the Eiffel Tower Restaurant was delicious, as I was famished by then. We kept all our conversation in French, and I did tolerably well, with his help. The view from that level was good, but I wasn't satisfied until I went to the very top, so we joined the crowds to the spectacular heights and gazed down at the entire city and environs. The only trouble was that it was raining by then, so it was less than perfect, as Ernst expressed it.

We went next to the Place de l'Étoile and up onto the Arc de Triomphe, which he opined as the best view of Paris because it was seen from the hub of the wheel, so to speak. It was superb, and I loved every moment we spent identifying all the landmarks.

Of course I had to go to Montmartre, where the first martyrs of Paris had met their death. Fortunately the rain let up as we ambled through the whole area and saw all the bawdy sights of the theatre district. Then we ascended the hill to the Sacré Coeur Basilica, and I exclaimed at its many-turreted white splendor atop the innumerable steps ascending to it. I'd studied it in Art History and now at last I saw it face to face. Ernst told me he was a hiker from childhood, so we climbed those hundreds of steps instead of riding one of the motors, and he far outdid me.

It was well worth the climb, for as we entered the church I was filled somehow with a sense of the real presence of Christ. The huge mosaic of Him over the center front nave with outstretched arms as though offering eternal peace, made me exclaim, now in English, "Oh Ernst, isn't it lovely? It just seems as though the Lord Jesus is here in some special way."

"I'm glad you like it, ma chérie."

"You know, I believe I like this one more than all the others we saw last year. St. Paul's, Cologne, Notre Dame, Florence and Milan Duomos, and especially St. Peter's, are magnificent!"

"To be sure, you can't compare this with St. Peter's. Nobody will ever approach the Sistine art and un-equalled architecture of Michelangelo's design in its dome, and all of its interior."

"No, certainly not, I don't mean to compare them in that way, and I loved St. Peter's best with the Pietà and the incomparable Sistine Chapel, but there's just something here. . . . Know what I'd love to do, Ernst? Let's come up here Sunday morning for worship! I'm not Catholic, but just this once I'd like to partake of the mass here, especially since I don't know offhand of any Protestant churches in Paris."

"Mamma mia," half under his breath, "I haven't been to mass since I was a little boy. It's impossible! I wouldn't know how to act." A twinkle came to his eyes as he must have seen the tinge of disappointment in mine, and he said, "Okay, mein Mädchen, so be it. Then after lunch we'll begin at le Louvre. You've told me you're interested in it, and it takes at least ten days to go through properly. So I suggest you take several Sundays for it, since it's free on Sunday."

"That's a good plan, for I'm very anxious to see the Louvre. Thank you, Ernst." I reached up and whispered in his ear, "I love being with you."

"La même, chérie," giving my hand a little squeeze.

We paused on the steps below the portico after we came out, and looked back at the lovely Romano-Byzantine structure, as I murmured the second verse of the Forty-eighth Psalm, "Beautiful for situation, the joy of the whole earth, is Mt. Zion, on the sides of the north, the city of the great King." This would surely suffice now for the real Mt. Zion.

The sun was trying to shine through fully overcast skies, and it was very humid, but the breeze on the hill was refreshing. There were quite a few fellows and girls sitting around on the steps singing pop songs, some with guitars, and I almost wanted to join them.

"You'd be surprised how many of them are Americans," Ernst remarked, following my gaze. "Let's sit down here for a few minutes and enjoy their songs, the breeze and view before going on down."

We could see the whole city stretched out before us in the distance. "I've certainly seen Paris today," I said, happily hugging my knees as we sat on the steps. "You're right about the best view being from the Arc de Triomphe, though."

"It's a matter of opinion, but I think many agree," he shrugged and said pensively. It struck me that he'd been just a trifle withdrawn at times today. Because of last night, perhaps? What was he really like beneath his very knowledgeable yet casual stance? Why did he cut me off yesterday so abruptly when I read the Scripture to him? Had I offended him? I prayed for wisdom and an opportunity to continue sharing my faith with him.

"So you're preparing for a career in architecture," I prodded. "What brought you to that?"

"Ah, probably because of various jobs I had for a time in construction. Then later, in summer tour directing, I had opportunities to see and study all these superb structures in detail. I'd like to have a tiny part in carrying it all on."

"That's cool, and you know so much about them. I got a lot more out of my art courses this year because of your interesting lectures last summer on our bus."

He shrugged. "A lot of it comes straight from the book I carry on tours, but I do need to refresh my mind and compile some notes beforehand. It's a nice job, but with all the numerous details of hotel and meal reservations, Customs, language problems, money exchange, sightseeing, entertainment and difficulties in general, it's exhausting business — especially with you Americans, if you'll forgive me!" He grinned as he lit a cigarette.

"I know what you mean: the ugly American. Our family tried not to be."

"You succeeded very nicely. I liked your dad. He seems to be a fun-loving fellow. Attractive too."

"He is. He loves life. Mother seems to hold down his enthusiasm for living at times. You saw him dance with the ladies at Tivoli. He's a keen executive. I wish I could be sure he's a born-again Christian," I sighed.

"How can you be so 'sure' anyone is a ... how did you say, 'born-again Christian'? A person does the best he can, and hopes for a good life. What need for more?"

" 'Born again' is a term meaning 'born from above' or 'born of God.' Jesus said in the third chapter of John that you must be born from above in order to be saved from the eternal punishment for sin. He also said later, 'I am the way, the truth, and the life; no man cometh unto the Father but by Me.' As I understand it, when you put your faith in Jesus Christ as your Savior from sin, He comes in and gives you His life. Actually the Holy Spirit of God lives in your body. That's what eternal life is. When He lives in you, you live forever, with Him. Death is only a passageway to a more perfect life than we can have in these bodies—Heaven, His presence. And you can't ever lose the eternal life He's given you when you receive Him as Lord. I could show you in the Bible where Jesus points this out, but maybe you'd rather I didn't. It took me a long time to understand that, even after I was saved, because my mistakes and boo-boos always made me doubt that He could still love me enough to keep me forever!"

"So! You seem quite positive you are going to 'Heaven.' "

"Yes, I am. Not because of any ability or good in myself, but because He gave me the gift of life and He's not going to take it back. He keeps His Word as a gentleman! He promises the gift of eternal life, His life in us, when we allow Him to enter our lives. You can have that gift too, Ernst."

"Ha, you make it sound much too simplistic," he said as he smiled. "I like my life as it is. I've got a lot going for me now, and a good future. Why worry about after death now? Let's start on down. There's lots more to see."

A tiny sigh escaped me as we stood up to descend the steps. "The benefits aren't just after death, chéri. Eternal life begins when you believe, and it's such a joy and comfort to have One always near when you need help, or just a friend, or protection."

"As long as you believe in your Christ, you can live like the devil and everything is okay, hm?"

"Well, no, not exactly. I mean, when you love the Lord and live for Him, you want to try to please Him in everything you do. Paul treats that subject in the sixth chapter of Romans."

"Ach, please, no more verses."

"I'm sorry. Why do you object to hearing or reading the Scriptures?"

He hesitated, shrugged his shoulders and said, "I don't know. Maybe it's because I feel you're trying to shove things down my throat."

God forbid, I thought. *Oh Lord, help me. I'm not getting anywhere, and it's discouraging.* Lamely I said, "I'm sorry, I certainly don't mean to do that, Ernst. Honestly." My breath was fast becoming gasps. "These steps! Let's slow down."

"Do you want to stop for a few minutes?"

"No, just go slower. Ernst, the reason I want to show these things to you, instead of just saying them, is to make you realize they're not just my ideas, but God has said them in His Word. Do you understand?"

"I'm sure lots of people have figured many different interpretations from the Bible. Yours is just one of many."

I wanted to shout, It isn't mine, it's His! He wrote it through holy men, He interpreted it to me, as to all His children, by His Holy Spirit, and everything in it is true and bears on the central message and meaning of the cross Jesus died on! But something told me I'd said enough. Cut it off, leave it for now. We were almost to the bottom of the steps. "I can feel the muscles in the backs of my legs tightening."

"You still want to do it again Sunday?"

"Yes, I do," I said gaily, looking back up once more.

"I'll make a hiker out of you yet."

"You must be a super one, from what I've seen, Mr. Neubauer."

"No, I'm not in nearly as good shape as I used to be. When I was a boy, I'd spend weekends with my parents hiking for miles, camping. Later in my teens, groups of fellows and girls would hike all over Austria all summer long. Great times. Ski in winter, hike and camp in summer. After my sisters were born, Reni when I was... let's see ... eight, and Anna when I was ten, Mother was tied down for a few years, and Dad and I went alone; but when they got old enough, we all again had two or three years of it before I began going with my friends."

"What fun!"

As we walked, he told me how at nineteen he and a few friends had left home to travel all over Europe, and soon had me drooling at his account of all the places they went.

"It's no big thing — just like you Americans traveling all over the States, into Canada and Mexico," he stated.

"But you're talking about *Europe!* How I'd love to go and see all those places!"

"Maybe you will, chérie." He squeezed my hand as he looked down at me. "I feel the same way about America. As I told you, I spent a short time in a few of its cities, three years ago, before I started summer tour directing, and I'd love to see it all too. Very natural."

"Ernst, I'm curious. Why did you *really* shave your beard?"

He laughed. "Actually, to please my tour people." I nodded in understanding.

Between short rain showers, we walked to the Madeleine, the Opéra, looked at Jean d'Arc's statue in gold and the Église Saint-Roch, and saw a few other sights of downtown Paris till the humidity and exertion tired us both. We had a late supper at the Café de la Paix and returned to the pension.

"Tomorrow I'll take you to the Rue du Faubourg St.-Honoré to see the most exclusive shops on planet earth, so it is said, but I don't promise to buy you any clothes!"

"Speaking of which, I need to get out of these sticky togs and into a welcome bath," I commented as we wearily ascended the last steps to our rooms. "I'm exhausted."

Later we talked a while in my room, and again he took me into his arms and kissed me persuasively. My negative response was only a little easier this time.

Apparently unperturbed, he turned and stood at the window, pensive again, looking out. Strangely, as I watched him, my mood of the morning returned. He's mature, sophisticated, intelligent and very attractive... I'm only one among many, I thought wearily. Questions filled my mind, doubts. . . .

He turned back to me, held my shoulders, gazed into my eyes and said, "Melanie, if you go with me and we stay in the same room, I will not touch you sexually. Do you believe me?"

Oh come. Not touch me, I thought. Sure, Ernst! But then as I returned his gaze, I actually believed he meant exactly that, for there was definite sincerity in his eyes. *Not touch me!* If I went with him, and tested his sincerity . . . *I* tested *him* — what colossal arrogance! If *I* tested *him* . . . could I keep up *my own* resistance? My eyes left his and closed tightly as I bent my head in shame, and the persistent question was repeated.

"Do you believe me, Melanie?"

Yes, yes, I actually believe you, I thought, but how can I answer? If I say 'Yes,' then 'What's the problem?' you will ask, and in your mind there will be no obstacle. Are you counting on my weakness when the time comes? *Or what are you?* Mistrust mingled with trust in my mind as the question hung in the air, and he would in another second lose patience with my hesitation. I must above all be honest. "Yes, Ernst, I do believe you, as absurd as it all is, but why place ourselves under such a ridiculous restriction? I can't trust myself. You may have strength, but I don't."

A quick smile crossed his eyes, as instantly faded. I thought I could read his probable thought: Ah, but you claim the strength of the Lord, Melanie! Where would that strength be then? Did I see sarcasm in his eyes in that instant? I thought blindly, I can't trust you, Ernst! You meant what you said, but only so far. Just the same, though I had won temporarily, I felt I had offended him, and his next words proved me correct.

"You don't really believe me."

I sighed and thought tiredly, Where is the meeting of our minds? We are on totally different planes. To you everything is physical, to me the most important things are spiritual. How can I tell you so you will understand, that exactly in this way Satan works? You don't even believe Satan exists!

He must have read my expression, for with a slight shrug of his shoulders, he said, "We have talked enough for tonight. Will you please try to believe my sincerity and ability to handle things? At the end of a tour day, I fall into bed exhausted. But to have you near me would be —

heaven. Think more about it. Goodnight, Melanie. I'll see you tomorrow." He turned and left me.

Just as he was opening the door, I cried out, "No, Ernst, the answer is no, and I don't want to talk about it any more!"

The look on his face crushed me: crestfallen, hurt, disappointed. I wanted to throw myself in his arms and shout 'Yes!' but a quick look of pride flooded his eyes and his jaw tightened as he turned and walked out of the room with a muttered, "To each his own."

Some residue of the day's frustration and fatigue caused my words to follow him, "I don't want to be another one of your *wives!*" But he was gone, and as I looked out the door after him, he never turned as he walked down the corridor. In gasping horror at what I'd said, I slammed the door and threw myself on the bed, shame and self-revulsion shattering me.

CHAPTER 5

I don't know how long I lay there, hating myself, crying inconsolably. Something so beautiful was now so ugly because . . . of what I had become. A year ago there was no conflict, at least until much later, but what he asked was now out of the question under any circumstances. Oh, *why* had I said what I did to him? Why hadn't I just declined graciously instead of acting like a shrew? I shuddered. There was no sound to indicate his return to his room, nothing but the rain pouring down outside, making the room even muggier than before.

I'm sorry, Lord, I've blown things. How can I even ask Your forgiveness? Turn away, I wouldn't blame You. . . . No, what was it Aunt Kate had said? When you make a mistake, His forgiveness is only a prayer away, because He loves you. . . . "When we confess . . . He is faithful and just to forgive. . . . If we believe not, *He* abides faithful. . . ." "I will *never* leave you. . . ."

Oh, Father, I'm sorry for what I said. I surely hurt him if he heard it. But what can I do about it now? Despair filled me.

Slowly a kind of peace was restored, and I knew there was nothing to do but go to bed and leave it all with Him. I saw my unfinished letter and felt like tearing it up, but resisted, and when I finally got in bed, it was a fitful sleep that came. Sometime hours later I wakened and saw it was only a little after three. The rain had slackened but was still falling. The whole hideous episode returned to mind, and I tossed until dawn when I finally drifted off again.

Hours later I wakened with a sinking feeling that everything was over between Ernst and me. Why should he want anything more to do with me? How could I ever face him anyway, and what on earth would I do? I didn't know a soul in Paris. I knew I'd have to face loneliness after he left on his tour, but I hadn't allowed myself to think about it. Certainly never like this! A horrible sense of loss pervaded me. Oh, Ernst! *Ernst!* After a whole year, this. . . .

I must apologize to him, I thought, *but how can I?*

A definite thought came. Go to his room. Oh no. No, I couldn't do that! Ugly pride rose in me. The inner voice repeated, Go to his room. I somehow knew it was the Lord's. *No, Lord, not that! Surely I'm the last person he'd want to — to barge in on him.* Insistently it came again: Go. . . .

Resignedly, I got up, dressed, tried to pray, but a recollection came to mind, ". . . if . . . thy brother hath ought against thee, leave thy gift . . . first be reconciled to thy brother, and then come and offer thy gift." It was incredibly hard to do.

With beating heart, I went out, and as I was locking my door, down the corridor a door opened and a couple emerged from their room. Startled, I unlocked my door again, slipped inside and waited a few minutes. *Lord, please don't let anyone see me knocking on his door and asking admittance!* I recognized an even uglier pride in myself, but repressed it. Again I opened the door, still made sure no one was in sight, locked it and went and tapped gently on Ernst's door. No answer. I tapped again, a bit louder. Still no sound. He isn't there! I thought in panic. *Where is he?* Once more I knocked, sharply.

A muffled sound came, "Qui-est-là?"

I sighed in relief, and stage-whispered, "Ernst, it's Melanie. May I come in for a minute?"

Silence. Had he heard? "Ernst —" I began, then heard a click.

A muttered "Come in" sent my quaking heart lower. Opening the door timidly, I entered and closed it after me. He lay in the bed, the wrinkled sheet pulled to his waist, otherwise probably naked, hair disarranged and a day's stubble on his chin. The close mugginess of the room held a stench of alcohol, stale tobacco and sweat. His clothes were strewn on floor and chair in disorder, a cognac bottle was on the table and butts cluttered an ashtray. He seemed to have difficulty focusing his eyes on me as he started to speak.

Resisting the impulse to turn and leave, I forestalled his words by saying quickly, "Ernst, I came to apologize for what I said last night. I'm terribly sorry, and I also said something awful after you left, which I hope you didn't hear."

"I heard it," he muttered with a frown.

"I'm really sorry about that, and I apologize," lamely. "I'm going now, and you just stay there and sleep, or if you like, I'd be glad to go get you some coffee or something, or just go away and stay."

For a few seconds he didn't reply, and I nervously began to pick up his clothes and fold them; then as he didn't object, I hung up his trousers and shirt. Something fell from one of his trouser pockets to the floor. It was a switchblade knife, I saw as I picked it up and replaced it. As I put his shirt on a hanger, my eyes smarted as I recalled all the joys of yesterday.

"Coffee sounds good. Black," he slurred. "Sorry — for the mess. Thanks for picking up."

"I'll get you some coffee. Be back later."

I went down to the lobby where Henri was behind the desk, and his eyes lighted up as he saw me approach. I noted the hearty appreciation of the Frenchman in his eyes as his gaze swept over me and he greeted me warmly.

"Bon matin, Mlle. Alexander."

I returned his greeting and asked if I could get some coffee. "C'est pour Ernst."

Instant sympathy and understanding filled his eyes as he spoke in French, "Ah, Ernst came in very late this morning."

"Would you tell me when, please?"

"About three, but don't tell on me! He was not in good shape. I've never seen him like that."

I hesitated, then said, "I was very ugly to him. . . ."

A slight smile in his eyes made me want to clear up a point, so I whispered, "And he was refused, twice, and so it will be, if. . . . Now, don't tell on *me*, please!"

"Ah." Enlightenment, a tinge of disappointment, then what I hoped was respect crossed his face. "I understand." He reached for the telephone, made a short call, then directed me to the dining room where coffee would soon be ready for me.

"Thank you, Henri. You're a good friend," I said as I left him, and felt his eyes on me as I started upstairs.

When I returned to Ernst's room with the coffee, he was sitting on the side of the bed with some clothes on, head lowered. He looked up at me apologetically as I gave him the coffee, saying, "Thanks. I'm sorry. I was a fool and drank too much. It doesn't happen often."

"Don't mention it, Ernst. I'm the one who caused it, and I — I have lots of things to do, and I want you to . . .

to . . . ." I emptied the ashtray as I wondered how to say *forget everything,* picked up the partially empty bottle to discard, then set it back down as I realized I had no right to throw the rest away. "I mean. . . ."

"Throw it out, Melanie. It won't do either of us any good." When I'd done it and started to leave, he reached for my hand. "Can we both try to forgive and forget? I'll be better after a while, and if you like, we'll eat lunch and then go on with our sightseeing. Before you came I bought tickets for a concert tonight by the Conservatoire Symphony Orchestra. All right?"

Relief mingled with remorse filled my heart, and my eyes misted as I nodded and said, "Yes, Ernst, yes, thank you," then left and returned to my room.

Halfheartedly I finished my letter with its belated confession to my parents without mentioning the present crisis, except to say, of course, there was no question of my going with him on tour. Then I wrote to Aunt Kate the whole account from the time we parted, and a couple of post cards to friends, did some laundering, then the phone rang. It was Ernst, saying he'd be ready to leave any time I was.

Somehow we got through the next three days, but there was a cloudy barrier between us, which I tried to ignore. More sightseeing, window shopping, the concert, a bateau-mouche ride and dinner up the Seine at a charming retreat, an afternoon in the Bois de Boulogne and one out at magnificent Versailles, and even an evening at the Follies Bergères failed to restore our former joy and excitement of first reunion. The nights for me were heightened only by the fact of his presence in the room next to me, though beyond my door, voluntarily locked to him.

Sunday, as planned, our last day together before he would meet his next tour group at Charles de Gaulle Airport, we returned to the Sacré Coeur for my first mass, ate lunch at a cafe near the Opéra, and spent the rest of the day at the Louvre. Weather-wise, the weekend was lovely.

Having mutually agreed on a rather quiet plan for our last hours together after the hectic day's activities, in early evening we strolled through the Tuilleries Gardens. I couldn't rid myself of the feeling that he would be relieved to get away from me, though he had kept to the plans to show me the city. Though the feeling made me a trifle ill at ease with him, I clung to the comfort of his presence, hating the thought of tomorrow's separation. Even though he would be in the city with his group for two days, they would be in another hotel, he would be busy with innumerable details, and probably our only contact would be by phone, if he chose. Gravely I wondered if he would even call me when his tour was over. Somehow it seemed that our separation would be a permanent one.

Our conversation was not very stimulating. Two subjects seemed mutually verboten: any allusion to his dead hope of my going on his tour, and because of a timid, perhaps guilty self-restraint on my part, the subject of faith in Christ. So we small-talked and dwelt on the artistry of the things we saw, skirting more personal subjects.

"I haven't given you any entrée to acquaintances to build friendships after I leave," Ernst said apologetically. My heart sank. Was this a put-off? "I really don't have friends here to speak of. Henri, yes, but —"

"It's nice to know he's around, and I'll soon be moving to the Alliance dorm and will make friends." I tried to sound light and cheerful, but I'm afraid unsuccessfully.

"You have no contacts at all around Paris?"

"No, but, come to think of it, there's a school — a Bible Institute — I've heard of in Lamorlaye, somewhere north of Paris, which I want to look up some time soon. A friend at my church at home told me about it."

He nodded with an almost imperceptible shrug and described how to get there, a matter of a thirty or forty minute train ride from the Gare du Nord.

Awkwardly yet sincerely I told him, "I wish I could thank you adequately for all you've done, and the lovely time you've given me, Ernst. I'll miss you very much."

Just a hint of sadness crossed his eyes, then came the standing reply, "It was my pleasure, Melanie." Was it real, or just politeness?

We sat down on a bench by the small lagoon in the gardens and watched the few children still sailing their little boats, and couples strolling about as dusk turned to dark.

The moment was nostalgic as I thought of the past six days we had filled to the brim with pleasure yet not without some turmoil. As though sharing my thoughts, he mused, "What's the old saying, about 'Life is hard to beat; you get a thorn with every rose, but ain't the roses sweet?'"

I smiled, for it was one of my favorites which I had written him in one of my letters. Leaning against him I whispered, "I honestly love you." He gently kissed my lips, then suggested we walk some more.

We crossed the Pont des Arts and strolled toward our haunt on the Left Bank along the Seine.

"What is love, Melanie?" he asked me rhetorically. "Everyone agrees, love is the big answer to life, but can it be separated from action?"

"To me, love is a beautiful concept, a gift of life, but I

don't see how it can be separated from action," I mused. "It's shown by many kinds of actions, though."

"You speak of love, and you've shown it, not in the way I desire, for to me it is at least in some part fulfillment of desire, but you are different, even from last year. You make me have to drink alone, even . . . just different. . . ."

Could this have been evident to him, I thought with joy. I spoke gently. "Well, yes, I am a completely new person from what I was, inside, as I've tried to tell you, Ernst. Even though sometimes, as you've seen, I . . . I make a mess of things — a real mess." Shame again made me shudder. "The little matter of the wine I've declined with meals is a small sacrifice to Him who bought me with His death and lives in my body; a purely optional, personal thing, for I used to enjoy wine, as you may remember. There are much more important sacrifices, and actually, obedience is far better than any sacrifice, except that of our whole selves to Him." I paused, then sensed an urge to continue. "But, back to 'love,' more important than its evidence in action, I think, is its Source. You can't separate love from its Source, which is God."

"Most religions in some way say 'God is love.' "

"Yes, but in Christianity, the whole gospel message is uniquely rooted in love. 'In this . . . this action . . . is love, not that *we* loved God, but that *He* loved *us* and sent His Son to be the propitiation for our sins.' " I thought, here I go again.

"A pretty little sermon," he said wryly, "for tonight."

A bright moon was reflected on the river, and stars sprinkled the night sky. We were near the spot where he'd told me he was not an atheist, and I started to speak of it, when he pulled me to him almost roughly and kissed me with a passion not yet evidenced.

It was harder that night than on all the former ones put together to refuse his love and thus fulfill his desire.

CHAPTER 6

Ernst called me from his hotel the night before his tour group was to leave, talked a while and offered to come over if I gave the word, but I knew how difficult it would be for both of us. I hated saying it would be better not to, for already my only comfort had been knowing he was still in Paris, and I missed him dreadfully, and told him so. After a long silence, he said, "Au revoir, chérie. I'll call you."

When, I wanted to ask, but resisted. "Yes, please keep in touch, Ernst. Je t'aime. Au revoir." I hung up slowly. Words can be so meaningless, I reflected sadly. Would I ever hear from him again? Once more I had refused him, and regret fought with desire inside me.

I had finished registering and other details at the Alliance on Monday, and done a lot of walking both days, trying to avoid the places we'd been together. Both evenings I'd eaten early at the pension and stayed in my room, hoping he would call. Only briefly had I chatted with Henri Monday morning, but hadn't seen him since.

There seems to be a merciful numbness to the kind of stress I was facing in his departure, for which I thanked the Lord, but I'd felt a strange lack of interest in reading the Bible or even praying. After his call, I sat thinking for a long time, then finally slipped to my knees as I realized I had put Ernst before the Lord in my thoughts and desires. Confessing to Him was hard at first, but He soon filled me with such a sense of His presence and comfort that it was a sweet reunion.

Then I realized I would have to make a choice. If I had lost Ernst and he would not return to me, it would be hard — terribly hard — but if he did come back, I knew now there would always be a conflict between loving him in whatever milieu and my fellowship with my precious Lord and Savior. If I wanted to remain fully in the love and fellowship of Jesus, I would have to be willing to give up Ernst forever. He had rejected the Lord who had saved me, by simply doing nothing about the claim God had on his soul, and as long as he reacted in the way he had, not acknowledging Jesus Christ as Savior and Lord, there was no life of God in him. He was spiritually dead, and I could only pray for him continually, but I would have to be willing to give him up.

Oh, Lord, I just can't do it! I love him so much, I cried. *Surely, Lord, there is some way. . . .* Then I thought of God's people, Israel, who in past ages were always compromising God's commands, and falling into sin as a direct result. No, there is no compromise. I must choose, I knew, but I didn't want to. *Lord, make me willing to follow Your best for me,* I prayed in a semi-submission, and with that I had to leave it. With that I wrestled in the first days after he left, missing him so keenly it hurt. I revisited the places we'd been, reliving our times together, and one day I took some paints, returned to our favorite haunt by the river and began painting the scene before me, dominated by the south view of Notre Dame. As afternoon wore on toward evening, the loneliness became so intolerable that I gathered my things and sadly rode the metro back to the pension. He had not called, nor did he that night.

I'd begun to hope for mail from home and to ask at the lobby desk, but not one letter had come, so I pulled out all of Ernst's old letters and re-read them. It made me alternately happy and sad, and very frustrated. In my Bible I found a piece of paper with some of the words of a song our church choir had sung a few weeks before I left home. A tear or two filled my eyes as I read:

Lead on softly, Lord; Lord, lead on.
In the unknown days to come,
When I may be far from home,
Will you lead on softly, Lord, lead on.
I must follow through the darkness; ...
        Lord, lead on.
Light for only a step at a time,
        Your hand on mine,
Follow through the darkness, ...
        Lord, lead on.
I must keep my eyes upon You, Lord; ...
        Lord, lead on;
Though my eyes be blind with tears,
When I cannot calm my fears,
I must keep my eyes upon You, Lord; Lead on.[1]

Tomorrow, I thought as I prepared for bed, I will take the train up to Lamorlaye, if only to get away from here.

Paging through Isaiah, I found two verses I had underlined several weeks before, Isaiah 26:3 and 4: "Thou wilt keep him in perfect peace, whose mind is stayed on thee: because he trusteth in thee. Trust ye in the Lord forever: for in the Lord Jehovah is everlasting strength."

1. Words and music by Maxcine W. Posegate. Copyright by Hope Publishing Company. Used by permission.

Lord, I prayed, *keep my mind on You, that I may have this promised perfect peace, the fruit of Your Spirit. Help me always to trust You in big as well as little things.* I prayed much for Ernst and my parents, that God's Spirit would even then be speaking to them, and reminded Him of the covenant that Aunt Kate and I had made. *But, Lord, make me willing . . . and keep me in Your strength. . . .*

The next morning, after reading through the Ninety-first Psalm, I checked departure schedules by phone for the train I would take, and gave my key at the lobby desk to Henri, who was just going off duty. I told him where I was going, checked metro directions, then asked, "What do you do now, go home and sleep all day?"

He nodded with a grin. "Mostly. Eat and sleep, then eat again, run errands, then come back to work. On my day off, or my night off, I have fun." A short pause, then, "I live in the area of the Gare du Nord; would you mind if I travel with you?"

"Not at all! With pleasure," I responded happily, pushing my hair back.

"I'll make sure you don't get lost in the metro! In fact, I'd be happy to put you on the right train, if it pleases you."

"You're so kind, Henri! Yes, I'll accept that offer, for I'm still not much at ease in the metro, and I'm unfamiliar with the train station."

As we walked to and rode the metro, I found out he was a bachelor living alone, and guessed he made a pretty fair salary. He seemed rather aimless, a trifle bored with life, and I ventured to ask, "What, no girl?"

"No special one — just girls," he shrugged, and the "des filles" told me the type he meant. I talked about Ernst, told him how we'd met and how I missed him, then spoke to him of my faith in Christ, and how God had changed my life almost three months ago, making so many things different. Henri seemed impressed, asked questions and was much more open, less intellectual than Ernst had been. I even translated some verses for him from my New Testament. He gave me all his attention.

Between the metro stop and the train station, he suggested we get something to eat, which sounded good to me, and we found a restaurant and ordered a late breakfast.

"I wish I felt less bleary-eyed, or I'd be happy to help dispel your loneliness," he said as we sipped coffee.

Smiling, I said, "I wouldn't dream of breaking any more into your needed sleep. I appreciate your time and help."

"Perhaps, another time. . . . "

"Perhaps, Henri."

When we parted at the train station, I was quite encouraged at our talk as he waved, saying, "Au revoir, Melanie. Passez une bonne journée!"

The European Bible Institute is housed in a spacious and very attractive chateau, I saw as I approached it from the gatehouse. I'd heard it had once been a palace. It was in flat, verdant country on the edge of the town of Lamorlaye, just south of Chantilly, where the train had stopped, and from where a taxi had brought me. The large circular drive led to the center entrance, with another entrance on the left corner, and on the right of the drive was a building which looked like a residence hall.

I knew that E.B.I. was the first of several Bible Institutes established in different countries in Europe by the Greater Europe Mission, an inter-denominational mission to European countries.

There were very few people in evidence around the chateau, except for a construction crew. It was Saturday, and I figured the semester had ended some days or weeks before. I asked one of the construction workers where I could get some information about the school, and he told me to go inside the left entrance of the chateau and up the stairway. I thanked him, walked over and up the steps.

Inside the building I ascended another stairway to a reception room and entered it. There were a few people standing in the hall talking, and I walked over to a girl seated behind a desk and asked her in French some questions about the school. Then I told her I was an American visiting Paris for the summer, and beginning Monday, a student at the Alliance Française. She expressed interest that I was American, and said she wished I could meet the Director, Mr. David Barnes, who was also from America. However, she regretted that he was on a trip to the States. Then her glance rested on two children who had just ascended the steps and who walked over and stood next to one of the couples.

My glance followed hers, then she smiled at me. "Oh! There is an American family, visiting the Institute today. They are missionaries who have been in France for several years. Would you like to meet them?"

I hesitated, not wanting to interrupt, but they were apparently finishing their conversation, for they said their good-byes to the other couple and turned in our direction. I told her I'd love to meet them, and repeated my name.

"Rev. and Mrs. Harding, may I present to you this young lady from America who is visiting Paris for the summer? Miss Melanie Alexander."

The gentleman, a tall, handsome man with wavy gray-brown hair, large dark brown eyes and a small cleft

62

in his chin, spoke first in English as he held out his hand, "How do you do, Miss Melanie Alexander? This is my wife, Laurie, and two children, Marguerite Anne and David."

"How do you do?" I shook his hand, then hers, a woman of grace and beauty with a warm smile in her deep blue eyes, and a certain bearing I always admired in girls taller than I. Then I nodded to David, who looked about fifteen, and to Marguerite Anne who was about Johnny's age. "It's so nice to meet some people who speak English! It makes me homesick," I said and smiled. "Especially with you two, for I have a younger brother who is twelve, and seeing you makes me miss him."

"I'm almost twelve, too," Marguerite Anne spoke up, "and my brother is fifteen." She was a beautiful child who I could see resembled both parents.

"Where are you from, Melanie?" Mrs. Harding asked.

"Richmond, Virginia, and I'll be at the Alliance for a while."

"Richmond? Oh Jim, did you hear that?" her eyes twinkled with delight as she looked at her husband and back at me. "We both graduated from the College of William and Mary in Williamsburg!"

"Really?" I exclaimed in amazement. I wanted to hug them both.

"Only a few years ago, of course," Rev. Harding put in with a wink. "This is quite a — no, I started to say, coincidence, but with the Lord, there's always a purpose. What, may I ask, are you doing here at E.B.I.? We're here with the idea of sending David, for a session at least, later on."

"I just came up to look around, and well, maybe meet some fellow Christians. I haven't found any like-minded folk after a week and a half in Paris." The receptionist had resumed her work at the reception desk, I noticed. "How long will you be around?"

"Jim is here partly on business for our Mission, and we're also enjoying a two-week vacation. We're missionaries with North Africa Mission, based in Marseille," Mrs. Harding explained.

Her husband suggested we walk outside, to look around, and they all nodded to the girl who had introduced us. I thanked her.

I told them more about myself without mentioning Ernst, as we strolled around the chateau, and I found out a little of their background and work. Rev. Harding was the only son of deceased missionaries to Algeria, North Africa, and Laurie was from Long Island, New York. He had had a pastorate for one year in Pennsylvania before they came over in 1958 as missionaries to the Muslims, many of whom were living in Marseille and southern France. Both children had been born in France.

I was delighted to hear of quite a few evangelical churches in Paris. Rev. Harding was to preach and his wife to sing at one of them the following morning. Most happily, I found out the location, how to get there by metro, and promised to come. They were all staying in the home of friends near the church, which was located in the Belleville section of Paris.

As we strolled by the little stream on the grounds, then over to the girls' dorm which Rev. Harding informed us had once been the palace stables, he would comment or joke every so often about something we saw. Once he stopped to ask some information about the Institute from one of the construction workers, who we found out were Christian fellows from America. Though I couldn't help feeling a little like an intruder, especially with the children, I was amazed at the way they made me feel a part of the family and shared so much with me.

After a while, father asked son if he'd seen enough and at his "Yes sir" we walked to their car, having agreed at their invitation "of course" to return to Paris together. My heart was singing a thousand rhapsodies, for I loved these people already. David was the image of his father, a bit gangly though not quite as tall, with longer brown hair, and rather well-mannered. Johnny would like him a lot, I was sure, wishing he were here to meet David. Marguerite Anne was a bit mischievous and interrupted a few times, reacting strongly to her brother's occasional teasing. In the parents there was a certain grace that indicated a close walk with and a deep love for the Lord. When we parted company in late afternoon near a metro stop, for I wouldn't let them drive me all the way, I promised to see them in the morning. They even offered, if I liked, for David and Marguerite Anne to meet me at the metro stop entrance about fifteen minutes before service time, to show me the way to the church.

"Oh, please let us!" Marguerite pleaded excitedly.

"Why, how thoughtful. Yes, that'll be fine. I'll look for you. Thank you very much. Au revoir!"

In my room after supper that night, I couldn't stop thanking and praising God for all His goodness and mercy in bringing this wonderful family into my life. I wasn't even tempted to think it coincidence that we all were at E.B.I. the same day at the same time, for I knew it was the Lord who brought us together.

CHAPTER 7

It was the first sermon I had ever heard in French, and most of it I understood with only a little trouble. Rev. Harding was a powerful, Spirit-filled preacher, and his sermon fed my hungry soul, filling me with joy, comfort and challenge. Mrs. Harding's voice as she sang "O Rest In The Lord" was one of the loveliest I had ever heard. Her rich mezzo-soprano tones and poignant quality were evident, her solo superbly rendered. How warmly the words spoke to my heart and renewed my trust in God. It was all from the Lord, I was confident.

After the service, to which the younger Hardings had brought me from the metro entrance, the people were very friendly. They had recently lost their pastor, M. Aaron Kayayan. The Hardings introduced me also to the friends with whom they were staying, M. Pierre and Mme. Yvette Debard, a very warm-hearted older couple, who cordially insisted, to my delight, that I join them all for dinner and the afternoon.

We had a jolly time and a delicious meal with which I helped the two ladies, my gray-haired hostess, short, bustling and eager to please, and Mrs. Harding, calm and efficiently helpful. The homey atmosphere made me a little homesick. When we'd finished the dishes, we sat out in their yard with the men and talked, of course in

French. They asked about my school plans and then about my home church, and I told them of my Methodist background, but that I had recently joined Immanuel Baptist Church in Richmond, which has about a thousand members. I added, "This church supports, fully or partially, almost fifty missionaries around the world."

"Excellent," M. Debard remarked, as the others nodded. "They must truly love Jesus Christ. We hope you will worship at our little church while you are in Paris, and come visit us often too."

"Thank you very much. I certainly would like to."

Marguerite Anne, who had been romping around the yard with the dog, now plopped down on the grass between her mother's chair and mine, breathing hard, and asked a question, "Do you have any other brothers besides the one you mentioned, or any sisters?"

I told her more about my only brother Johnny and that I had no sisters, then said, "You have a very pretty name, Marguerite Anne. I like it."

"Thank you. But I like to be called Marg." The others smiled at her frankness, and David snickered, at which she wrinkled her nose at him.

"She was named for her two grandmothers, but she never knew them, nor they her," her mother said sadly. "Both Jim's parents, whom I never met, died suddenly of pneumonic plague in Algeria while Jim was in college at Wheaton in Illinois. It was a tragedy, because they were such fine medical missionaries. Jim tells me I shouldn't call such things tragedies, because they come to us through God's permissive will, but it was tough on him. My own mother, Marguerite Reynolds, died before we were married, of leukemia."

"What a shame, for both of you." My eyes misted as I thought of my parents.

"Jim transferred to William and Mary that fall for his senior year, and we met there. He brought me to faith in Christ."

"How neat," I said, fascinated.

"I was just there when she made her decision for Jesus Christ," Jim interposed, running his fingers through his hair. I noticed a look of love pass between them, at what was undoubtedly a special memory.

"He started a campus Bible study group which later affiliated with Inter-Varsity Christian Fellowship —"

"Really? We have a great IVCF group at Westhampton-U.R., which God used in my life! But go on, please."

"Well, for several years after his graduation — he was a year ahead of me — we lost touch, until God brought us together again at his first and only U.S. church in Stevensville, Pennsylvania. Soon after Mother's death that spring, Jim was used of God to bring my father to the Lord. . . ." Nostalgia filled her eyes, then she smiled. "He's since married again and been a real source of joy and provision to us. Retired now, though still active."

"David was named for both our grandfathers, David Alfred," Marg put in, and her father nodded, then murmured something to his son. David punched his sister and suggested that they do some throwing, and Marg ask me, "Would you like to throw a frisbee with us?"

Surprised that what I thought only an American sport had caught on here, I smiled and said, "Sure, I'd love to," and the plastic disk soon appeared. We tossed it awhile, then the two men joined us for some exercise, while the two ladies conversed. Some time later, M. and Mme. Debard excused themselves with profuse apologies, to take a short rest.

"The trouble with old age!" The Frenchman shrugged with a laugh, smoothing his ample mustache.

"We wouldn't know, Pierre!" Rev. Harding teased his friend, then more seriously, "I may do the same after a bit."

Mme. Debard, in her cordial way, again urged me to make myself at home and stay for the evening service, but I told her I'd better get back before dark and do the rest of my packing for check-out and my move to the university in the morning. Again I thanked them for their hospitality, in case I left before they finished resting, and promised to return to the little church.

"Stay as long as you can and talk more with us, Melanie," Mrs. Harding invited when they had gone in, adding, "Even though it isn't always 'done', please call us Laurie and Jim. We're just ordinary folk, and we want you to consider us your friends. We also want you to come down any weekend we can all arrange and visit us in Marseille."

"Oh thank you! You are more than kind. I'd love it!" Since the children were still playing, I grasped the opportunity to tell them about Ernst and my parents. Somehow they inspired my entire confidence, and I trusted them completely. They listened intently as I left few details out, recounting as nearly as I could my conversations with Ernst on religion and finally requesting their prayers.

"You do have a burden," Laurie said gently. "I sort of sensed you had something on your mind. We'll certainly join you in prayer for your family and Ernst."

"He seems to have done some thinking, perhaps more than you may suppose, even though he was hostile," Jim said. "But you planted some good seeds, and the Lord won't let them be wasted. There may be some problems in his personal life he hasn't told you about, which could

70

present difficulties. Of course, you know as well as I that it's far from easy even to think about the tremendous change Christianity demands. We face this constantly in our work, particularly with Muslims."

"Yes, I do realize that, and I'm sure you've had lots of experience, working with all kinds of people."

"And you don't want to be deceived by a superficial change, though Ernst sounds like a person who wouldn't pretend to so something he doesn't mean. Am I wrong?" Laurie asked.

"No, I think so too, but I'm prejudiced!" I said, thinking it a perceptive observation on her part. "I wish you both could meet him."

"I'd like to very much," Jim said, "but we'll have to wait and see how things go. If we're still here when he gets in touch with you, contact us and we'll do whatever we can."

"*If* he gets in touch with me," I said gloomily.

"I'm quite sure he will," Laurie consoled me. "He seems to love you. I don't see how he could help it!"

"Say, do you know about Eurofest to be held in Brussels in late July?" Jim asked, running his fingers through his hair. "European Christians are organizing a youth convention to which they expect thousands of young people to come from forty countries all over the world."

"Yes, I've heard of it and seen it advertised. I believe Billy Graham will be one of the speakers." I'd wished several times there were some way I could go.

"Maybe that could be in the picture somewhere," Jim remarked. "It may be for us. We don't know for sure yet. Something else occurs to me. Have you thought about getting a Bible printed in German as a possible gift for Ernst?"

"Oh, that's a great idea!"

"He'd get much more from one in his own language,

assuming that he would begin to read it sometime. You can probably get them in a book store in Paris. If not, let me know, and I'll get you one. At least he'll have one available if and when God's Spirit gives him the urge to read it."

"That's excellent, Jim. He sees every angle." Laurie smiled at me, then continued, "Melanie, one tiny suggestion. We're well aware of the lowered moral standards in today's world, but with your changed location, it may be a good time to be with Ernst in places other than your room — if he returns, of course. That's entirely your choice, naturally, but it would be better on several counts. . . ."

"Yes, I see your point, and you're right, of course. Less temptation and a better testimony," I agreed, thinking how amused I would have been at such a suggestion a few months ago. "No more problem anyway, for they're quite strict about non-visitation rules at the Alliance. Men and women, though in the same building, are on different floors, but are at least supposedly kept separate."

"Good. Most important, prayer will be our strongest weapon from now on," Laurie said, looking at Jim. "Right, dear?"

"It sure is, and I suggest we have prayer together now," Jim said. I nodded, and he led in prayer which filled me with a strong sense of God's presence, comfort and love.

Marg and David came back from their play and I soon thanked them all again and said my farewells. We exchanged phone numbers and I left them after making sure of the way back to the metro.

The next several days were filled with moving, getting settled into my dormitory room, and beginning my

French classes. I made a few friends, enough of whom were Americans to make me feel quite at home, but we were all too busy to spend time together other than back and forth to classes and meals at the Alliance cafeteria or the coffee bar for snacks. The Hardings had mentioned an Inter-Varsity Christian Fellowship group at the university, but so far I hadn't found it.

My cash was decreasing, and I consulted the university employment office about a part-time job. He said there was very little available unless I would settle for babysitting services, but would let me know if anything came up. Meantime, I told him to put me on the list of sitters.

Tuesday evening I called Henri at the pension to inquire about any mail and was overjoyed to hear he had forwarded a letter to me from Richmond, but there was no word from Ernst.

Next day I checked at the post office and picked up the letter, which was from Mother, and read it avidly. Not much out of the ordinary as far as news, except for one item which excited me. She wrote that a lady from my church whose daughter was a good friend of mine had called on Wednesday and asked about me, and she had told her of my cablegram of safe arrival. Mrs. Baber told her she would announce it that night at prayer meeting and they would pray for me. She then invited Mother to come with them to church Sunday if she wasn't going to her own church, or to the evening service if she was. I made a quick calculation about their prayers at church. Wednesday was the night I had spoken the awful words to Ernst that made us both so miserable and ruined our last days together. A strange answer to prayer, indeed, I thought with a touch of irony. Then I recalled the time difference and realized their prayers had been too late to prevent my temper flare-up, if they could have anyway, but no doubt they helped to sustain me afterward, and certainly the next morning.

Mother's letter continued, "Well, as you know, our church attendance hasn't been much to brag about lately, but I decided that I'd like to go with her, especially since they take such an interest in my daughter— whom I miss very much, incidentally! So I'll probably go. Maybe Dad and Johnny will go too."

Oh, praise You, Lord Jesus, I breathed with deep joy. Wonder if they went, and if so, how they liked it, I thought. Johnny had gone with me a few times, and they had all gone once when I was baptised by immersion before joining the church. *Thank You, Lord, that You're working!*

Saturday morning I went to a book store and found I'd have to order a Bible in German, which after only a second's hesitation I did, in faith that if I never saw him again, I could send it to his home as a memento of our friendship. On impulse, I bought a French New Testament for Henri, thinking some time I'd take it to him and have another talk with him about the Lord.

On my way back to my room, checking at the post office, I found there were three letters for me — ironic how they came in clusters — from Dad, Aunt Kate, and Ernst!

CHAPTER 8

Tearing open Ernst's letter, I found it a tantalizing disappointment, but read it over six times before I let out a long sigh as I leaned against the wall with mixed emotions. It read:

1 July, 1975.

Dear Melanie,

Sorry there's been so little time to write. We left Florence this A.M., staying in the same hotel where you had your 21st birthday "party" last year. Just returned from escorting the group to Piazzale San Marco, Venice. What a blast. I miss you.

Wish you could fly over and spend the day with me tomorrow. I could show you the real Venice — all the fascinating little byways. Too bad.

We fly from Amsterdam to London, Friday. Plans after that uncertain.

Yours,

Ernst

I couldn't see much between the lines as I walked back to the dorm. What a difference from his former letters!

Miss you, but I'm doing fair without you, it seemed to say. Me too, Ernst, but I'm not doing very well, I thought as my dark glasses fortunately hid tear-filling eyes. *Lord Jesus, please fill my being now, so I'll be willing to do without him, for I know that's what You want. You want all of me, Lord. That's the way I want it too....*

When I got to my room, even before reading my other two letters, I knelt by my bed and poured out my heart to God. *Lord, take me, all of me! I submit to Your Lordship, and I claim the fullness of Your Holy Spirit. He's yours, Lord — I claim Ernst for You, and I give him up to You. If You want me to break up with Him, I will. Only save him, Lord, bring him to Yourself, for Your glory alone, if it takes years. I'll pray for him always, for the rest of my life, no matter what.... I love You, and I thank You for whatever You do through me, Lord Jesus....* Tears filled my eyes as I gave up my life and my future to my Saviour, and a sweet peace and deep joy filled my whole being.

Quite a while later, I read the other two letters. Dad sent money, "just in case," and wrote that the three of them had gone to my church Sunday, and quite a few of the people had given them a warm welcome and invitations to return. The sermon had been excellent. Johnny was playing little-league baseball regularly. Mother missed me so much that she cried more easily than usual, had gotten upset over the awful Eastern Airlines plane crash in New York City, in which over 100 people had died, but he was keeping her as happy as possible with lots of going. He thanked me for the "confession" about Ernst, said he'd figured out the situation pretty quickly, but now trusted me completely and even admitted saying some prayers for me. His expressed trust was precious, and the prayers were a big hurdle for him to admit, I knew, and I prayed again that he'd go all the way to the Cross of Jesus Christ, and find the close relationship with Him that I had found.

Aunt Kate wrote all kinds of encouragement, good news and assurances of her regular prayers. *Thank You, Jesus, for Aunt Kate!* She had set up her trip to include Brussels during Eurofest the last week in July, suggesting we plan to go up from Paris together, at least for the weekend of July 25-27, or as long as I could manage it. The trip would be her birthday present to me. "The city will be pretty jammed, for they expect almost 10,000 young people to come from all over Europe and North America — to witness to Jesus Christ! Hallelujah!" she wrote. "I've recently become acquainted with a man who will be involved in Eurofest, so, who knows, maybe we'll get together an hour or so while we're there!" That sounded very interesting indeed.

I was so happy and excited that I just had to call Laurie Harding and talk with her. Mme. Debard said they'd just returned from sightseeing, but called Laurie, who said talking with me would be a pleasant relaxation for her.

"How have you been this week, Melanie?"

I told her briefly of the week, then of the letters with their varied news.

Of Ernst's letter, she commented, "It sounds good and bad. We'll double our prayers for him, and praise Him now for His answers, however they may come."

All of a sudden I had a feeling of such deep gratitude that my throat tightened. These people are so understanding and helpful, just as concerned about Ernst and me as I am! "Laurie, it's amazing to me about your positive attitude right from the first, about Ernst. Neither you nor your husband expressed a negative thought at all."

"Melanie, dear, we love you in the Lord! You're a precious girl. Please don't ever feel that you're a burden or a bother to us, even if we ever seem to show it, for we make mistakes just as everyone does. Missionaries wear no halos, you know! Believe me, I know how it is to be so far away from home with no friends but one or two. You and I both want to see Ernst saved, and when we pray for someone's salvation, we can be positive it's God's will, for He's not willing that *any* should perish, but that *all* may come to Him. So we *know,* sooner or later, if it takes years, He's going to answer! The Lord has proven this truth in our lives many times. But as you surely know, intercessory prayer must precede and surround any witness, if it's going to be effective. Though that sounds rather humanistic, we believe it's the key. Do you agree?"

"I sure do and have prayed for him for almost three months," I said. "Laurie, there's something more, too. I've just had it out with the Lord in prayer. I . . . gave Ernst up . . . to God —" Swallowing hard, it was difficult for me to go on.

"Oh Melanie, bless your heart. I know that wasn't easy for you. You're braver than I am."

"It was very hard, Laurie. But He gave me such peace and joy!"

"Yes, He does! This is what our Lord wants: full surrender of ourselves — our most precious possessions and deepest desires. I *know* it wasn't easy, but the Lord will give you much grace, because probably what's ahead will be even harder. You'll be tested, and Satan will fight it. Please forgive me for being so frank, for I know you so little, but remember, the Christian life is a spiritual warfare."

"Yes, that's what Scripture says."

"Be much in the Word, Melanie. Read it faithfully every day."

"I will. Thank you so much for your counsel and encouragement, Laurie. Is Jim going to preach again tomorrow?"

"Yes, and you already have an invitation to eat with us at the Debards'. I wonder if you'd like to spend the afternoon at the Louvre, since you mentioned wanting to return. We'd like the children to see it again too."

"That would be super, and please thank Madame, and tell her I'd love to be with you all again for dinner. You're all so wonderful."

"You know we'll be returning to Marseille a week from Monday. Next Sunday will be Jim's last day to supply preach. We'll see you tomorrow morning; all right?"

"I'll be there early. Bye now."

Sunday, Laurie sang another beautiful solo, Jim preached an excellent sermon, and the Communion of the Lord's Supper was especially meaningful and precious as I renewed my vows of full commitment to my Lord. After dinner at the Debard home, we enjoyed the treasures of the Louvre together and parted in the late afternoon, almost the close of a lovely day.

Filled with a creative urge shortly after we parted, I got out my paints, walked over from the dorm to the river and proceeded to finish the view of Notre Dame I had begun a week and a half before. Working contentedly, I was able to put on final touches before dusk fell. Then I headed back toward the Alliance, rejoicing in the Lord and the wonder of His creation and marvelous presence. Many couples strolled along the Boulevard St.-Germain, and sidewalk cafes were crowded, music sounding forth as I rambled by.

Much of a rainy Monday I spent writing letters and cards and reading my Bible. Tuesday being only partly cloudy, after classes I donned jeans and tennis shoes and decided to take my sketch pad and go up to Montmartre to sketch the Sacré Coeur Basilica. Strangely, the thought came that I was doing the places which had been very special to me because of Ernst. Maybe I'll show them to my grandchildren, ha! I thought ironically, as I tell them of all my lost loves.

Once again after a somewhat tiresome climb up the hill from Montmartre, I decided to mount the steps to the broad stone platform about halfway up to the Basilica for a better vantage point. As I walked up I remembered the first two times I'd been here with Ernst. How thrilling the first jaunt that second day in Paris, and how rather depressing yet pleasant the second trip that first Sunday morning. . . .

I found a place to sit a little below the platform so as to include it in the sketch, from which I hoped later to paint a picture, and began working.

So intent was I that I didn't notice the passage of time, nor at first a man who paused to look at me, then at the picture, then sat on a bench not far from me. So many people were descending the steps that I paid scant attention to him until I seemed to feel his eyes on me. Glancing over at him, I thought him vaguely familiar. Probably I'd seen him the evening before on the quay by the river or in St.-Germain. He wasn't attractive. There was a large purple area half covering the upper side of his gray-black bearded face beneath a partially bald pate. He seemed about average weight and height.

I kept sketching, trying to finish, but a wary feeling crept into my stomach and I realized clouds had thickened, hiding the sunset, and dusk would soon turn to dark. Though a bit disappointed that I hadn't quite finished, I suddenly decided to leave as I noticed the crowds had thinned considerably.

When I reached the bottom of the steps I glanced back up, but couldn't see anyone sitting on the bench. A few people were still coming down, and he must be among them somewhere, I figured, relieved that he was out of sight. Surely if he knew me, he would have spoken, I thought with slight concern.

Somewhat hungry, since I'd had no supper, I found a small eating place with quite a few people in it, went in and ordered Coke and a sandwich. Tearing off my sketch from the pad, I looked it over critically, then put it in my small shoulder bag.

As I left the little restaurant I regretted the time taken to eat, for it was pitch dark, storm clouds had lowered, and a not too distant clap of thunder sounded as I hurried toward the nearest metro entrance. It was getting too late for a girl to be out alone in Paris.

The lights inside as I descended the metro steps were a welcome relief, and I hoped I'd reach my dorm before the storm broke.

Pausing at the direction signs to be sure of the right level of my train, I glanced around and saw him. The same man who had sat up there at Sacré Coeur watching me was moving directly toward me. Few people were around, and this time a faint smile played about his bearded mouth as he suddenly reached out to me.

CHAPTER 9

Realizing in horror his intention, I jerked around and fled down a flight of stairs and ran left along a passageway where I saw a knot of people ahead. Glancing behind me as I caught up with them, I failed to see him, and sighed in relief, but where was I going? Surely not the right train. For another short flight down I stayed with the small crowd, and onto the platform where a train was just coming to a stop.

Suddenly I saw the man coming from another direction toward me! How in the world...? But he knows his way and I don't, I thought in panic, as I found a door and entered the car, praying the doors would close before he reached one. It was almost full of people, and I found a seat at one end where I could see the whole car. Sure enough, there he came walking toward me and sat down on a seat not six feet away, facing me.

Positive now of my danger, and not wanting to show any recognition, I noted the line we rode, then rummaged through my bag and pulled out my metro map to find where I was going. It was not only the wrong line, but was taking me the opposite way from my planned destination.

Dear God, help me! Help me! What does he want? Stupid question. What should I do? If I'd scream, they'd all think me balmy, for I couldn't prove a thing. I must get off this car, but how? I studied the map and found a way to get back to the right line, if I could run fast enough. Just to make sure, I mapped out an alternative way, thanking God for every bit of direction both Ernst and Henri had given me.

Just before the train stopped, I bounded up and past the man, dodging around people to reach a farther door, edged around the others exiting, and ran as fast as possible for the nearest stairway, not daring to look behind me. If I'd seen a gendarme, I'd have gone straight into his arms, but I had no time to look for one.

Finding the right line was much harder than I'd calculated, and I had to return by another train to reach it, but when I finally found the right level and approached the proper platform, I glanced around warily at the faces of the evening crowds. Near the tracks several yards ahead I saw the back of a familiar man, and beside him stood a younger fellow who suddenly pointed at me. As he turned his head, I recognized my pursuer. Instantly I darted back up the stairway, desperately hoping he hadn't seen me.

How did he get there? Could he possibly know where I was going? And are there *two* after me, or am I losing my mind, I thought incredulously as I ascended two steps at a time. The only recourse was to take a familiar route and hope for the right train to hide me from them.

It would be a risk and a long ride, but it would take me to Henri *if* it wasn't his night off, at my former pension on the south side of the city. I hurried toward an oncoming train and saw with relief it was the right one, jogged along it till it stopped and the doors opened, entered and sat in the least conspicuous seat I could find, panting heavily. The car was much emptier than the others had been, and I prayed my pursuer had lost me. As we came to each stop, the passengers left, a few at a time, and I began to wonder if I would be left alone in the car. Suppose they were on the same train. What would I do? Four more stops to go, the last two above ground, then the two block dash to the p—

Just then the door at the opposite end of the car slid open, and to my horror, he entered and saw me instantly. Between us there was one passenger, a man, facing me, and I sprang up, walked toward my pursuer and plopped down in the seat directly facing the lone passenger. Apparently my tracker was caught off guard for an instant by my action, and sat down a few seats away as the train slowed to its next stop.

Glancing at the rather seedy looking man in front of me, however, I wondered if I had made a mistake. If he were drunk, I'd be lost; but almost worse, he proceeded to make an obscene gesture to me, and my heart sank. Suddenly glancing at the door my relentless chaser had just come through, I noticed with terror the fellow who had pointed at me to the first one back at the other platform. His eyes were on me as he entered the car and sat down.

I was lost. *Lord, for whatever comes, I'm Yours, and I know You'll be with me. . . .*

The train was now going above ground, and I gazed out the window to see if it was still storming and saw with relief that it was just drizzling. The streets would be wet, and between my stop and the pension there was the unlighted canopied section of the outdoor sidewalk market on the side of the street I had to go on. I recalled with dread how dark the half block was where I'd have to go, with two men undoubtedly in pursuit.

Flesh creeping, I felt the eyes of three men on me as the train stopped and soon started again. Next stop was either my escape or my end. A plan formed, poor as it was, and I waited in suspense till the train stopped. When it did, I suddenly pointed at my pursuer and shouted at the man in front of me.

"Please, keep him from catching me!"

Bolting for the door behind us just as it opened, I sped down the steps and dashed through the exit to the street. I could hear them behind me, and a car approached just as I began to cross the street.

Straight in front of the headlights I darted as brakes screeched and the car swerved and skidded to avoid me. I heard a hideous shriek behind me as though someone had been hit, but dared not look back as I raced through the blackness under the canopy toward the street leading to the pension. Footsteps still sounded behind me, and I knew at least one was still in pursuit.

Panting for breath, I turned up the street and saw my goal almost a block away with its lighted open entrance. Glancing behind, I saw with terror he was almost on me. No one else was in sight.

"Help!" I screamed, "Help me — Jesus!" Could I make it? A superhuman spurt of speed carried me to the entrance as I realized the man had stopped chasing after my scream, and I stumbled into the lobby crying, "Henri!"

Henri was coming out from behind the desk as he saw and heard me, but there were two others in front of the desk, and as they turned toward me, I saw through tear-blurring eyes, one of them was a girl and the other was Ernst!

CHAPTER 10

"Ernst!" I screamed and almost fell into his arms.

"Melanie! What happened to you?" I felt myself shaking, panting and sobbing at the same time. Then I noticed the girl standing next to him was looking at me with what seemed amused interest, and Henri stood near her with intense concern on his face as my glance reached him. "Tell me, Melanie!" Ernst said sharply.

I gasped, "A man — two men — followed, chased me — tried to — Oh — all the way from Montmartre — Sacré Coeur — through the metro —"

"What did he look like?" Ernst demanded.

"Part bald, gray-black beard, medium weight, height —"

He looked thoughtful, then alarmed. "Did he, by any chance, have a port-wine-red stain on the upper part of his face?"

"Yes!"

A muttered curse escaped his lips as I saw him look at the girl with fury; then he gently pushed past me, went and hurried out the lobby entrance, his hand taking an object from his pocket. A spring released a switchblade, and I weakly cried, "Ernst. . . ."

Quick as a flash, Henri was out the doorway after him, and I sank onto the nearest chair, dimly aware of people appearing in the lobby, questioning, and more sharply aware of the girl, attractive and tall, like Ernst, at the desk too casually lighting a cigarette, watching me. Who was she? What was she to Ernst? She answered no questions, just shrugged at someone's inquiry.

Suddenly we all heard sirens in the distance, and I groaned as I recalled the shriek behind me as I ran across the street. Police, ambulance!

"Oh!" I gasped, my head in my hands, "Have I—? Is he *dead*? Have I killed someone?"

The few people in the lobby dispersed, some out the entranceway and toward the metro line, from where louder sirens sounded.

A few minutes later Ernst strode in the door, followed by Henri. Ernst came to me and said, "I'll take you back to your dorm at the Alliance." Not at all averse to that, I nodded gratefully, thanking the Lord for my safety and provision.

He ordered Henri, "Call a taxi, and give her a room," nodding toward the girl. My vast relief at mention of a taxi changed to apprehension at his words. He approached her and muttered something in what sounded German. There were sharp words between them, and though his back was toward me I heard a note of threat in his voice.

Glancing at Henri behind the desk as he put down the phone receiver, I saw disapproval on his face; then he came over to me and said with sympathy, "I'm so sorry for what happened to you, Melanie. There was an accident near the metro stop, and a man is badly hurt."

"Is he *dead*?" Ernst came over to us as Henri answered.

"No, but of course they aren't sure of the outcome yet."

"The driver—?"

"Melanie, are you all right?" Ernst asked with concern as Henri shrugged and I nodded doubtfully. "Please forgive my poor manners. Ilse, this is Melanie Alexander. Melanie, Ilse Muller, a friend from Austria."

Ilse approached, saying, "How do you do?"

I greeted her, trying to be more charitable than I felt, for there was something about her casual manner that turned me off, making me wonder with sharp dread and hurt just what her relationship to Ernst was. Then the realization hit me of the awful sight I must be in my jeans, shirt and tennis shoes, my mussed hair pulled back in a pony-tail. I apologized for my appearance, adding, "Guess it was good, under the circumstances, that I wore these," and went on to describe something of my horrid experience.

Before I got very far, Henri saw and indicated that a taxi had just pulled up in front, and Ernst said quickly, "Come, Melanie, let's go. I'll see you later," to the others, with a meaningful glance to each, and we left the pension with few more words than necessary.

In the taxi I felt very ill at ease. So many questions filled my mind that I couldn't even ask the first one. I must have been in some kind of shock, for I could hardly collect my jumbled thoughts.

Ernst's face was extremely troubled as he looked at me. "Melanie, I'm terribly sorry. If anything had happened to you . . . Mein Gott!"

"Well, you couldn't — It wasn't your fault, after all."

He gazed at me as if he wanted to say something but decided against it. Instead he smashed one fist against his other palm, squeezed his eyes shut with a black frown and muttered, "What a wretched, rotten fool I've been."

Something in me snapped. "Look, I don't get it. I've had a frightful experience, and you sit there saying what a fool you've been. What's that got to do with it? There are so many things I just don't understand!" My eyes began to fill with tears and I turned my face toward the window, ashamed at such weakness. "Sorry."

Compassionately, he put his arm around my shoulders, drew me to him and laid his cheek on my head, cradled against him.

"Melanie," he murmured, "I don't deserve you."

Stifling a sob, I couldn't speak for a minute. I was supposed to be doing without this man, had given him up, and yet the comfort of his nearness was too much for me to pull away from. Two tears fell.

"Cry, Melanie, go on and cry. You need to. Here," he gave me his handkerchief. "You've been through so much — for me," he uttered with a tone of chagrin.

After drying my face, I gave it back and said, "Thanks. Please tell me about the accident. It — it was my fault, Ernst! I ran right in front of a car as I dashed across the street, and it must have hit one of my pursuers."

"*Really?*" Amazement widened his eyes, then the stricken frown again. "Mein Go—"

"Please don't say that again."

"Sorry. You might have been... I... we didn't stay long enough to find out much. I was looking for someone else. A car had turned half around, against the other curb. A man lay a short distance from the car, evidently thrown by it, and a small crowd had already gathered. Someone said he was still alive, and the driver still in his car. We didn't stay to see more. Evidently no car had been coming from the opposite direction, fortunately. It'll be in the morning papers."

I shuddered at the thought of it all. Where was my tracker? "Did you see what the injured man looked like?"

"No, I didn't recog — didn't get a good look. So our bloody scoundrel is still loose. If I'd found him, I'd have kill —"

"Don't! I'm glad you didn't find him. Surely you wouldn't . . . . But, Ernst, *is he going to keep after me?*"

Again the black frown. "Not if I can help it."

After a pause I asked shyly, "Who is Ilse?"

He searched my eyes, then squeezed my shoulder a bit. "Please don't be concerned about Ilse. She's just an old friend. A part of my past, which is dead, forever." Under his breath I barely heard, "I hope."

When the taxi let us out, Ernst came into the dorm lobby with me and said, "I'll be in Paris for a few days. Till Monday. When are your classes out tomorrow?"

I told him my schedule and he said, "Please stay as close as possible around here. Don't go anywhere else alone. May I have the privilege of taking you to lunch tomorrow?" A sheepish grin spread over his face.

After a slight pause, I said, "Yes, of course. Ernst, thank you for bringing me home, and for your letter. It meant so much."

He sniffed and shook his head apologetically.

"Oh," I said quickly, "would you like to see my sketch of Sacré Coeur which I made before all the excitement? I must have lost my pad in the melée somewhere. Good thing I put the sketch in my bag. Here it is."

Examining it, his eyes softened and seemed to mist a bit. "It's beautiful, Melanie. You're a real pro. I'm tempted to ask for it, but have you other plans?"

"I wanted to paint a picture from it, but. . . ." I shivered involuntarily at the awful memory. "I'd rather you have it if you want. It's not at all good, though."

"Thank you, chérie. I shall treasure it always, as I treasure your love."

Feeling temptation, I turned away, saying, "I'll see you tomorrow then, and thank you, Ernst."

"Goodnight, Melanie," he said quietly, as I started up the stairs with a backward wave and glance.

The morning paper had a short account of the accident on a back page. The driver had minor injuries and the pedestrian was still in a coma from a concussion. I shrank from the thought of doing anything about it.

After class I hastened over to the bookstore to pick up my order. As I looked at the German Bible and the French New Testament, I wondered if I dared take the latter to Henri, ever. Instead I jotted a short note to him, enclosed it in the front cover and asked the salesgirl to wrap and send it to him. She gift-wrapped the Bible for Ernst after I'd written a little message to him on one of the flyleaves. Then I paid her and returned to meet Ernst, stopping first at the post office, where I found a letter from Mother.

It was her answer to my belated confession about Ernst, and was full of motherly counsel, which seemed rather irrelevant to my present situation, but for which I was grateful. Letters from home are very precious, I thought as I read on.

What came next really thrilled me, for she wrote how much they had enjoyed the service at Immanuel Church, so they had gone again the next Sunday, partly because Aunt Kate had come down for the weekend. The choir had sung Macfarlane's "Open Our Eyes" beautifully, the sermon had convicted her, and she'd returned with Aunt Kate for the evening service. Excitedly I read that she'd made a decision before the Lord, "with some help from Sis," to yield herself to Him. "Already I've realized a release from anxiety and tension and the joy of an actual personal relationship with God in Jesus Christ. It's amazing and wonderful, and from what you've told me, you know exactly what I mean, darling."

"Hallelujah!" I said softly, though wanting to shout. "Praise You, thank You, Lord Jesus!"

"You look very happy today," a familiar voice greeted

me as I looked up in surprise to see Ernst coming toward me. "Considering last night, you are positively radiant!"

"The skin of his face shone when Moses came down from the presence of God!" I cried happily, then quoted " 'As cold waters to a thirsty soul, so is good news from a far country'! Ernst, *my mother* has submitted her life to Jesus Christ as her Saviour and Lord!"

CHAPTER 11

His face revealed a combination of puzzlement and interest as he said, "It's certainly affected you well. I haven't seen you so happy since our first day together." A shadow crossed his eyes, then a faint smile. "I'm envious!"

Ignoring the quip, I scanned the rest of the letter and exclaimed, "Aunt Kate and I have been praying for this for months! God answers prayer, Ernst! Isn't it marvelous?"

"I suppose so." He seemed only slightly impressed. "You haven't mentioned Aunt Kate for a long time. Tell me more."

I told him about her and her part in Mother's decision, and our plans for the trip up to Brussels for Eurofest in late July.

"What is Eurofest?"

"European Christians are organizing a Christian youth convention in Brussels, and something like ten thousand students are expected to attend from all over the world."

"Ten thousand? Quite an aggregation." He seemed very impressed.

"It's such a joy to know there are that many young

born-again Christians who would come together in Europe." I noticed his nod of surprised approval.

While eating at a sidewalk café on the Place St.-Germain des Prés, we talked of reports of the accident, his trip and my classes, partly in French, and he noted the improvement in my accent. Then I took my gift out of its bag and handed it to him.

"Here's a little something I'd like to give you in token of my deep gratitude for all you've done for me, Ernst."

"Thank you, chérie." His face mirrored wonder as he unwrapped it. When he saw what it was and read my inscription on the flyleaf, his eyes softened as he smiled at me. "You are very kind and thoughtful to do this, Melanie. Thank you very much."

"May it come to mean a great deal to you."

"It will, to be sure."

"Well, I can't take credit for thinking of it. Some very dear friends I met here in Paris while you were gone gave me the idea."

"Oh? Tell me all about it."

I recounted my trip up to Lamorlaye and all about the Hardings and my two Sundays with them at the Debards', omitting only my telling them about him. He was amazed when I told him they were missionaries, and was even more so about the visits. He showed real interest in the Hardings' past experiences.

"I'm glad you found such congenial friends, Melanie. How fortunate for you."

"They've invited me to visit them in Marseille whenever I can, too."

"Well, you really made a hit with them!"

"No, it's just that they're so neat. I want you to meet them, Ernst. You'd like them a lot."

He shrugged. "It suits me. I appreciate their kindness to you."

"Since they're still in Paris, suppose I call them, and perhaps we could visit them this afternoon. Do you have any other plans?"

He hesitated only a second. "No, only to keep an eye on you, mein Mädchen!"

"Bless you, Ernst. I think it will be quite a while before I travel by metro again, alone."

"You did admirably in eluding them, but yes, please, no more evening jaunts at least!" Frowning, he added gravely, "One grab of your wrist, and he'd have had you. A tiny needle to put you out, then he'd pick you up and take you some place. . . . No one would get involved."

I shuddered in horror, but he said more lightly, "It's over, Melanie. Don't let me alarm you. Please forgive me." Concern filled his eyes.

Forcibly diverting my thoughts, I said, "I'll call them." He nodded, and I left to make the call.

Marg answered the phone, and after our greeting each other, she said her mother was there. When I talked with Laurie, she told me they would all be "at home" later on, and would be delighted to see us. "Madame may be resting, but do come about three, if that suits, and we're very anxious to meet Ernst," she assured me.

Ernst was rather pensive as we strolled, and I wanted to ask him many questions, and did ask a couple, but his answers were evasive and he seemed vaguely troubled. I was noticeably nervous as we finally descended to the metro, and he took my hand reassuringly as he smiled.

"You must try to forget, and resume your usual routine — when I am with you!" I grinned at his attempted humor as I glanced nervously around. At least it was a lot cooler underground, a relief from the hot spell, unusual in Paris.

It was a few blocks from the metro stop to the Debard home. After we knocked, Jim opened the door.

"Good afternoon, Melanie. This must be Ernst. Do come in."

"Yes, thank you. Ernst, this is Rev. Harding. Ernst Neubauer."

"Call me Jim, please. We've heard interesting things about you, Ernst." They shook hands as Ernst greeted him. Laurie came, welcomed me and turned to Ernst as Jim said, "This is my wife, Laurie."

They exchanged greetings, and I could see approval in Ernst's eyes as Laurie invited us to sit down and graciously opened the conversation. It wasn't long before Marg and David appeared, were introduced, and soon iced punch was served by Marg.

"You'll just have to hear about my horrible experience of last night! I even almost made the newspapers!" With all eyes on me, I pushed my hair back and launched into my "nightmare" with its surprising yet felicitous ending of finding Ernst at the pension. I told them too about the accident. Their faces all expressed concern, and Ernst's was very grave. Of course, I omitted any mention of Ilse and my devastation at seeing her with Ernst.

"Needless to say, we praise the Lord for sparing and protecting you, as He evidently did, especially on that last sprint when you called on His name," Jim noted as the others expressed agreement. "Calling on the name of Jesus surely does rout Satan and summon angels."

"That was really cool, hollering to Jesus for help," David said with admiration lighting his face.

"I'll say! Wow!" Marg exclaimed.

"Yes," I nodded. "I can sure witness to His powerful help. Ernst noticed how nervous I was today as we came over here by metro."

"It was a ghastly scare, to say the least," Ernst added bleakly.

"Wasn't it strange that they almost seemed to know where you were going at one point?" Laurie asked.

Glancing at Ernst, I saw him suddenly blanch, then nearly upset his glass as the now familiar black frown appeared. Though puzzled at his reaction, I quickly changed the subject, telling them of Mother's letter with its super news, at which they all rejoiced.

We talked for some time, and at Ernst's inquiry Jim explained his work with North Africa Mission, overseeing correspondence courses and Christian radio broadcasting to Muslims in France and North Africa.

"You must come to Marseille one day soon and see us. I'll take you to headquarters," Jim offered, running his fingers through his hair.

Laurie asked Ernst if he would be in Paris on Sunday, and he replied, "Yes, I have a tour beginning Friday, but we don't leave Paris till Monday morning." She told him about the church and that Jim would preach, and invited him to come, as I nodded hopefully. Ernst saw my nod, grinned and answered, "I see Melanie probably plans to go, and I think I can get away from my group long enough, as they'll be with a local guide till afternoon. As I told her, I intend to keep an eye on her as long as possible!"

"Good for you," Laurie said. "Melanie, can you plan to come to Marseille the following weekend for a visit? I suppose you'll be many miles away, Ernst, or I'd include you."

He nodded, thanking her just the same, and I eagerly accepted, knowing how much I'd want to get away from the hot city and loll on the beach a bit for a change. We agreed to make more particular plans later.

"Excellent, and we'll take good care of her, Ernst," Jim said with a twinkle. He mentioned Eurofest, and as Ernst expressed a real interest, explained more of the details to him. Ernst said he had been curious about Billy Graham for a long time.

"Maybe you could attend yourself, Ernst," Jim mentioned.

"Hm. I doubt it, but it's a thought," Ernst answered pensively.

Jim said they were pretty definitely driving, but couldn't leave before Thursday the 24th and would get to Paris that night. "We'll miss only part of the first day of Eurofest. May we pick you and your Aunt Kate up early Friday morning?" he asked me.

Tentative plans were made, though I told them we had planned to go up by train. I'd have to return for classes Monday or Tuesday, though Eurofest would continue all that next week. Jim gave us both some folders with information on the Fest.

After a while as we were leaving and Laurie and Marg were telling me something, I noticed Jim addressing Ernst. I murmured to Laurie, "I'll call you later or in the morning. Keep praying."

"But of course, dear. We'll be out tonight, so we'll talk tomorrow."

Impulsively I hugged Marg, who said, "I'm glad you can come see us. We know a grand beach to swim at!"

"I'm really excited about it. Thank you so much." I couldn't resist giving Laurie an affectionate hug.

"Love you," she said warmly. I waved to David and shook hands with Jim.

After we left, I asked Ernst, "Aren't they nice?"

"Yes, I'm very impressed. He invited me to lunch with him tomorrow, and when I hesitated, he said he'd get his wife to contact you and get with you somehow. He thinks of everything," he grinned wryly.

"That's really cool! I know you'll enjoy getting to know him."

"He's different. Vaguely reminds me of someone I know . . . a Christian."

We visited the Petit Palais to see the exhibition of the Swiss painter Henry Fuseli, then strolled toward the river. Somehow we ended up sitting on the embankment at the river's edge, our old haunt. It wasn't much cooler, but it seemed a little so, as the sun's bright rays lessened.

"I'll have to show you my picture I painted here while you were gone," I said, remembering my first loneliness and then later my joy in submission to the Lord the evening I finished it. Just three days ago, I marveled. Submission, yet what were we doing here together? It seemed so right.

"Yes, I'd like to see it," he said, then was silent as he lighted a cigarette and gazed across the water. Finally he sighed and spoke. "Melanie, for a long time my thinking has been taken up with rather superficial things, yet important: which career to choose, how to make money, have fun, and so on. Deeper matters have been rather submerged, except for an agreement with current ideas along political lines."

As he paused, I wondered what he was leading up to. "Yes?"

"For instance, naturally I've desired to see improvement of the deplorable conditions of our world, and I've felt a good answer lies in a different system. So, obviously, I feel our present system and conditions must be changed. Do you understand? Our political, economic, and social order should be completely overhauled."

"Well, we certainly have a lot of shameful conditions in the world, I agree, but it's taken the best minds of our parents' generation and of ours to try to change them."

"I'm sure you and I have different ideas about solutions. You've acquainted me with yours. Let me give you a picture of mine — at least till lately, the last couple of months," he said as I nodded. "I'm not at all certain that most statesmen and politicians really want to change national and international situations enough to do much about them. Responsibility for social and economic conditions is too deeply entrenched in present governments to improve them really, and at the rate it is being done, if at all, it would take centuries. Do you agree?"

"Mm, go on." I began with dread to perceive his thinking.

"So, to attain real peace, a much better way is to overthrow the present system and begin anew! Look at China today. Consider all the vast social improvements made in recent years by Communism. Even here in Europe, more and more elections are being won by the Communist Party: in Italy, here in France, and there's a strong element in Portugal, too, as shown recently. I have observed that revolution against existing political systems has worked quite well."

Feeling most intolerant, with difficulty I held down a rising indignation. "Speaking of China, Ernst, I'll admit propaganda has reported many social improvements. But I happen to know that in every Communist country, probably even China, in spite of their national laws of so-called religious freedom, Christian men are being mercilessly tortured, and imprisoned. Their families are left to starve because of no income, and their children pressured in schools to agree and adhere to atheistic ideology. State churches are mere political fronts. The only bright spot is that the Church, the body of Jesus Christ, is being strengthened in its faith by persecution in these countries." Another thought occurred to me and I continued, "And now the newspapers reported a while back mass executions and half-buried bodies of Cambodians by the new regime! *This* is your revolution, Ernst? I prefer spiritual revolution! But did you mention a change in recent months in your thinking?"

"Partially. Actually seeing and hearing reports of the mass exodus of Vietnamese in April — people literally running and climbing on airlift planes and naval vessels to get out of their own country — did rather begin to disillusion me."

"Exactly! I should think so!"

"Melanie, I must confess to you something." His troubled frown and the look in his eyes alarmed me. "I can't tell you much, but my thinking and ideas have resulted in some involvement. Because of this, Melanie, *you* were endangered last night! As you suspected, your pursuers knew not only your destination, but your exact situation!"

CHAPTER 12

I stared at him dumbfounded.

"But why? What did they . . .? Who are they, Ernst?"

"Please, try not to worry, Melanie. The bearded fellow I knew, but not the other."

"You *knew* the bearded man?" I asked.

"Yes. I can't tell you much, except that I'm relatively sure you won't be in danger any more, at least after I leave Monday."

"Ernst, you *must* tell me more! Who is this man, and what would he have done to me? And who and where is Ilse? Does she have anything to do with all this?"

He sighed and told me, "Ilse checked out of the pension this morning, and as far as I know, she has left Paris." Hitting his upper lip with his fist, he muttered, "Forget them, if you possibly can. And please, Melanie, for my sake, *please* don't go to the police. That's all I can say."

No more could I get from him as hard as I tried. Exasperated, I demanded, "Ernst, do you, or did you actually condone what's been happening in Vietnam, Cambodia, Ireland, and now in — *Are you a Marxist?*"

With a very faint smile, he answered, "No, I am not, technically. I do not possess the little Red Book or a card. Only in partial sympathy, as I've explained. Now, I don't know. And I find myself in the bad position of trying to extricate myself from past involvements. Other things, too. . . ."

"It's all too vague. Are *you* in trouble, Ernst?"

"It doesn't matter about me. No, it was all persuasive tactics. Please, no more."

I felt completely frustrated, helpless. Bending my head in my hands, I murmured, "How is it that when you love someone, it's so hard to believe evil of him?" I answered my own query, "That's the nature of real love, I guess, as the Apostle Paul said . . . ."

He was silent. Glancing at him as he gazed across the water, I suddenly felt a deep compassion for him, and I wanted to reach out and caress his cheek.

Instead, I pushed my hair back as I recalled something, and said gently, "It was over there that you told me you weren't an atheist. Of course, you could hardly be a Marxist if you believe in God, could you? Will you tell me what brought you to acknowledge Him?"

With a shrug he said, "I just never turned completely from the idea of God. My idea, that is. I've only been turned off by religion — people, I guess. Morals of a corrupt society."

I ached to help him. He needed a mature faith in a Person, the Lord Jesus Christ. Again I prayed in my spirit for him.

"I don't blame you for that. Empty, meaningless religion turns me off too, but knowing God's Son, the Lord Jesus Christ, really turns me on."

His dark glasses kept me from reading his expression too well, but he raised one eyebrow and looked away with what I thought a touch of wistfulness. Yet it seemed as though something was holding him back.

A thought occurred to me and I said, "A few days ago I finished reading a book I think would open your eyes, Ernst, as it did mine. I was reading it before I left home, and I brought it with me to finish. It's *Czech Mate*, the account of David Hathaway, a British Christian who owned a travel tour agency and was a Bible courier through a couple of Communist countries. He was finally caught in Czechoslovakia and imprisoned for ten months in their hellish prisons, just for carrying Bibles into a country which *says* it has religious freedom and *says* it even prints Bibles! Would you be interested in reading it?"

"Yes, I suppose so. Sounds interesting."

"I'll get it from my room when we get back. Maybe we'd better start back soon, Ernst." Shadows had lengthened and the sun had disappeared to the west of us. I suddenly grew apprehensive and stood up quickly, glancing around.

He got up, looked down at me, and slowly drew me to him. The feel of him against me was a protection I suddenly craved, wanted. . . .

"Do I have to ask you for a kiss, Melanie?"

I looked up at him and he kissed my lips tenderly, tentatively, until I pulled away with a guilty feeling of betrayal in my heart.

"Please don't, Ernst." I turned, not wanting to face the look of dismay in his eyes. The conflict in me was surely hurting him, and I hated to hurt him. I walked away toward the steps, and he followed in silence.

A few minutes later he said, "I know you're concerned about seeing your pursuer again. If he ever shows when we're together, not that I expect it, let me handle him. *Don't* call a gendarme, please. He's my problem."

I glanced at him in wonder and nodded, fervently hoping it would never happen.

After eating, dutch at my insistence, at the Alliance cafeteria, we settled on meeting about midafternoon the next day. As we strolled back toward my room, Ernst remarked, "You've changed, Melanie — probably with good reason. I suppose you feel you can no longer trust me. Guess I can't blame you."

What should I say? Was this the time to tell him of my decision to part with him? I shrank from it, yet it wasn't fair to keep silence. The divergence in our backgrounds, ideology and standards, to say nothing of beliefs, was so wide that I doubted we could ever make it together, even though we loved each other. Yet I did trust him, for hadn't he been honest with me, if only partially? But how, after all this time, could I possibly brush him off when I didn't really want to? I justified myself by thinking there'd been no opportunity.

"I do trust you, mon chéri, and I'm grateful to you for everything you've done, and — and told me."

"You sound as if you're about to call it quits," he spoke disconsolately. "I hope not."

My heart said I hope not, too, while my spirit said perhaps it would be best. *Oh Father, increase the faith You've given me to believe You will save Ernst! Otherwise, I must call it quits, sooner or later, or get in deeper.*

"I hope not, too, Ernst, for I'm praying for you, that you'll open your heart to Jesus." The words just tumbled out.

With an impatient sigh, he said, "It just isn't that simple, Melanie! Too many problems!"

We were at my dorm. I was tense, felt myself bad company, and needed to be alone. I told him I had some things to do, true enough.

"If you'll wait here, I'll go up and get that book for you and be right back." He nodded and I went up, found it and brought it back to him, saying, "You can put it in the bag with your Bible, and read them both!" With trepidation, I suggested, "You might try John's Gospel first, if you decide to read in the Bible, but of course that's up to you. Ernst." I reached up and caressed his cheek. "I honestly love you."

"Thank you, chérie, for that and for these. I'll spend tonight reading, and missing you." He kissed me softly, then tenderly touched my face as his gaze lingered on mine. "Je t'aime." My lips formed the same words, then I turned away as he said, "See you here tomorrow before or by four."

Before classes in the morning, I called Laurie and invited her to lunch somewhere nearby, as I told her Ernst had again cautioned me please not to go far from the Alliance.

"I'd love to, Melanie; I was going to call you. I'll come partway with Jim, who is to meet Ernst uptown, but we'll meet at your dorm and go from there, all right? It's strange that he's so concerned, but we'll certainly do as he asks. See you shortly after twelve."

Over lunch we got to talking about ourselves and our problems.

"I think it's really neat getting to know you and your family," I told her. "You're the first missionaries I've ever known, and it's interesting to see you have problems just like the rest of us."

Laurie smiled. "Oh yes, we surely do. As I've told you before, we're very human, with no halos; we face frustrations of different kinds every day and live just as much by faith as you or anyone. Missionaries, however, are very dependent on other Christians, and initially swallow pride because our living depends on the prayers and giving of others, humanly speaking. It works both ways, for we all as Christians serve Him in our separate paths, and we 'sent ones' pray daily for those who support us."

"I'm realizing that part graphically," I said, "as you pray for me, and Ernst, and my parents."

"I just hope that you see Christ in us. That's all that matters, for He's very real to us in all our difficulties. Take Jim, for instance. He's an excellent preacher because he has an outstanding vision of the Lord, but he has annoying habits like running his fingers through his hair, to mention a very small thing! Often I annoy him too, and I get annoyed at the children and fuss at them, which I know is wrong. Jim gets up-tight about the settled attitude of some older folk. So do I. 'It's always been done this way' — that kind of thing. It's not easy, but His grace is sufficient, and He works in spite of us." She paused. "Jim *loves* to work with young people. Sometimes I think he'd like to have been a basketball coach! Kids love him."

"Yes, I can see how they would. He's neat."

"France is a very difficult field, too. Over nine tenths of the people are so disillusioned with religion (Catholicism and Islam) that it takes years before we can build up rapport with them so they'll have any confidence in our gospel. This again is only the human side of a ministry. So often Jim has come from his prayer time with red eyes, blowing his nose, because his burden for the French people is very heavy, and we both need reminding that Jesus told us His burden is light."

"Hm. And you. I bet you sacrificed a great possible career in music with your beautiful voice."

Self-consciously she said, "Thank you. My parents felt the same way, but, Melanie, I've told myself and

Him many times that He gave me this voice, and I want to glorify Him alone with it, as with all His gifts."

"That's what we all should do. And really, all that we have comes from Him." I thought of my art, wondering how He could use it, wanting Him to. "I want Him to use me as He does you and Jim."

"He will, and He *does*, Melanie. Right now, He *is*. You've already been used by God to be a blessing to me, and you'll be a blessing today and later to Ernst, and others, and *His* is the praise! He'll *keep* using you too, as you submit to Him."

We talked of plans for the next two weekends, and after lunch we had prayer together up in my room, rejoicing and praising God over Mother's salvation, and praying for Dad, Johnny, and mostly for Ernst. She was as mystified as I was when I told her the things Ernst had said about Communism and his "involvements," but she sympathized with his concern over my safety.

Having several matters to attend to, she left about two, and I wrote a letter to Mother and Dad and one to Aunt Kate, did some studying, and got ready for Ernst. It was almost four when I decided to go down, mail my letters and meet him in the lobby. The Museum of Modern Art was showing a collection of drawings and sculptures by Henri Matisse, which I planned to suggest we go see. Since Ernst wasn't there yet, I decided to drop my letters in a mail box not far from the dorm, thinking I'd probably see him going or coming, and wondering at his lateness.

Having mailed them, I took a shortcut back, hoping I hadn't missed him. Between two buildings I suddenly caught sight of two men fighting. With a quick double take I recognized the one, partly bald and bearded, as my pursuer, and the other was Ernst!

Horrified, I started to scream, then clapped my hand

over my mouth as I ran toward them, then stopped as Ernst, seeing me, yelled, "Go back to your dorm! *Go back!*"

Hesitating only a second, I saw him pull his knife from his pocket and switch the blade, but the other man grabbed his hand and pushed him down as they grappled for control of the knife. Terrified, I turned and darted back, just in time to keep from almost colliding with a stranger coming around the building.

"Help!" I screamed, not stopping as I raced toward the dorm. Get a gendarme! *No,* Ernst had said not to get a gendarme! Approaching the dorm door, I saw two fellows coming out.

"Please help!" I cried to them breathlessly. "There are two men fighting back there with a knife! Please help! One of them is my friend!"

"Where are they?" one of them shouted. Praise God, they knew English! I was too excited to speak French.

A few others approached. I pointed and then led them back toward the buildings I'd come from, all of us running. "Around there!" I stopped, pointing ahead, suddenly even more afraid, as we rounded the building. The two fellows and a girl I recognized as a classmate approached cautiously. Everyone else seemed to have disappeared.

"There's no one...yes, there is!" I heard, sick with fear. "He's knocked out. The other guy must have split."

I moaned as I ran to the still form of Ernst, blood from his slashed shoulder staining his shirt, his white face and one hand. I bent down.

"Ernst! Oh, Ernst," I cried, as one of the fellows took out his handkerchief and laid it on Ernst's neck and shoulder to help stanch the blood. The other fellow gave me his handkerchief, and I gently dabbed away the blood on his face, tears filling my eyes.

"Please," I said to them, "he warned me of this, and asked me not to get the police. Can you help move him to the dorm?"

Ernst opened his eyes, slowly focusing them, then winced and gasped in pain. "Ernst, here are some fellows to help you. Looks like your neck and shoulder are cut pretty badly."

"Scoundrel!" he muttered, trying to get up. "Ach! Dizzy. Must have hit my head."

"Come on, old chap, we're going to help you up. See if you can walk, all right? We'll prop you up between us." He was definitely British.

"Sure do thank you fellows," I said, feeling quite helpless.

"Come on, man, easy now. That's it."

"I'm okay. Ach!" They got him up and supported him as they slowly began walking back to the dorm. "Appreciate this," he gasped with tightened jaw.

His sport coat lay on the ground, and I picked it up, guessing he'd been carrying it in his way, hooked over his index finger, when he'd seen the man.

The girl walked beside me, murmuring, "Quel dommage!" I asked her how and where we could get bandages, and she offered to go ahead and get the First Aid supplies out and have them ready. I thanked her gratefully and she hurried on toward the dorm.

Soon we had him on a sofa in the dorm lobby as near the washroom as possible. Fortunately I'd taken a First Aid course, and with the help of the others I removed his shirt, treated the ugly though not deep wound and bandaged him. It had been a narrow escape, for he told us the man had tried for his neck. Part of the neck had been cut, but miraculously, I thought, behind the vital carotid artery. With the clean damp cloths Jeannie had brought, I gently bathed his face and hands.

Shortly, Jeannie and the fellows, Rick and Warren, left after making sure Ernst would be all right. We both thanked them profusely.

When they had gone and we were alone, Ernst looked at me with a crooked smile on his bruised face, gritting his teeth with pain.

"I hurt all over. Thank you, chère amour, for helping, and doing as I asked — no gendarme."

"Oh why, Ernst?" I wailed. "How did it happen, and *why no gendarme?*"

CHAPTER 13

With a grimace he said, "When I saw him hanging around much too close to your quarters, I told him off and to stay away from you, threatening certain action if he didn't lay off you. Then for what he did to you Tuesday, I socked him and made him madder. Started to use my knife, but didn't. He's a better fighter than I, so when I saw you I knew he'd get me and probably you, so I got out my knife to protect us both. You know the rest."

"You might have been *killed* for me, Ernst."

"I brought it all on myself, Mel. It's over now. He got my knife, but. . . ."

"There was another man I almost ran into. Who was he?"

"Don't know, but I suspect they were a team. Good thing you screamed and ran. That probably made them leave, and saved my wallet." Another grimace. "Right now I'm more concerned about tomorrow. I'm in no shape to meet a tour group, and frankly, if I don't get back soon to the pension, I feel like I'll pass out. My head is splitting too."

"How? Shall I call Jim Harding to come and drive you there?"

"No, just call a taxi, please. I'll make it. Have him come to the back. I'd feel better if you stayed inside."

"Is there anyone who can take your place in the morning? Henri?"

"He's capable, but it would have to be someone from my agency. They're usually equipped for emergencies." I went and phoned for a taxi, came back and sat on the floor next to the sofa where he reclined.

"Melanie," he said with an effort, "you're tops. I've given you a bad time. You deserve a better deal. When I feel better, tomorrow or Saturday, we'll talk. I promise you."

"Oh, chéri."

"I read your book last night. You're right; it's an eye-opener. Also a little in the new Bible."

"I'm so glad, Ernst!"

"Jim and I had quite a talk today. Soup to nuts, so to speak. He mentioned a book I'd like, too. Something like *Living Dangerously*. Very apropos, right?" He grinned and I shuddered.

"Yes! Don't recognize the title. If you read it, pass it on to me."

"He's really sharp. I like him more and more. There's something about him, Melanie, that I can't describe. He must live very close to God."

Praise You, Lord Jesus! "I know, Ernst. It's just something of Jesus you see; I do too. You should hear him preach."

"Ach, right — I said I'd take you to church Sunday. *That* should be an experience! I've never been to a Protestant church service. Only for you," he grinned.

"Thank you, Ernst. Hope you can go, and enjoy it."

He glanced down at his torn, bloody shirt, saying, "Shirt's shot."

Looking closer, I too saw the slash was beyond repair, and thought tenderly, how dear even his shirt was, blood-stained and torn, for me. Resisting the impulse to

116

touch it, I reached for his sport coat, fondling it a second. "Mustn't forget this."

The back door opened, and we heard, "Taxi! Someone called for a taxi?"

Getting up quickly, I called, "Here we are. You may need to help him."

"It's all ri—ach! I can manage," Ernst said, getting up with difficulty. "I'll call you later, chérie." He kissed me at the door, and I watched them go with much more concern than I showed.

Then I went upstairs to the hall phone and called the Debards. Jim answered, and I told him all about the fight.

"Great Scott, that's a terrible shame! I'm really sorry, Melanie. We had a good long talk today. Never know what a day may bring forth, do we?"

"You're right. He said you both talked about lots of things. Could you brief me if you're not too busy?"

"Not too busy at all. We touched on deism versus a personal relationship with Jesus Christ, evolutionary humanism and some of the work of Dr. Henry Morris and the Institute for Creation Research, and quite a bit about the second coming of Christ. Serious talk, Melanie. He's really keen, and though he's resisting, I feel he may be seeking the truth, which encourages me a great deal. Now I know how to pray. But he does have problems to overcome. Big ones, though not too big for the Lord."

"He spoke to me of some kind of involvements which could cause trouble. Did he mention any of that to you?"

A pause. "Yes, he did, Melanie, but I feel that I should let him tell you when he chooses to. Frankly, he said he didn't want to upset you more than he already had. I know this tries your soul, but hang in there, and keep praying. He hinted at, or at least I inferred a little fear on his part, of losing you."

"Bless his heart. That would be very hard for me,

though it may have to come to that. I'm so concerned, Jim."

"We are too, honey. And now more so, with all this today. I sure hope he's going to be all right."

"Hope so too. I think he's still planning to take me to church Sunday, though he's getting a friend to sub for him tomorrow."

"Good on both counts. Satan tried his best to block the former. We'll be praying that the Lord will reach his heart, convict and convert."

"Right! Thank you, Jim, and I'll do the same and look forward to Sunday. Bye for now. Love to Laurie and all."

Two phone calls came for me that evening. The first was from Ernst to tell me he got back all right and had made arrangements with the agency about meeting his tour group at Charles de Gaulle Airport in the morning. As it happened, the group was to come to Henri's pension. To my relief, he said he was in bed and going to sleep as soon as possible.

The second was from Henri, who was again on duty at the desk. He told me Ernst had called him at home about the incident.

"You did a good bandaging job on him, Melanie. I think a good night's sleep and a day's rest will do him a lot of good," he said.

"Thank you. I'm sure it will, too. Hope it all heals well."

"Say, thank you very much for the little Testament you sent me. That was most kind of you, and I appreciate it. I'll think of you as I read it."

"You're very welcome. I'd hoped we could have another opportunity to talk as we did that Saturday morning, but there's been no time."

"I have a feeling we'll be more in touch, Mlle. Melanie.

Ernst says he wants me to keep an eye on you after he leaves. I don't know whether he should trust me or not!"

I laughed gently. "I'm quite sure he should, Henri. Sure do appreciate your concern for him. It means a lot. Well, enjoy your reading!"

"It's nothing, my good friend, and I shall. Good night."

A while later as I was reading, there was a knock on my door. It was Jeannie, who came in and asked how Ernst was. I told her and again thanked her for her help.

"Are you going to be here this weekend?" she asked, and I nodded. "You may be about the only one! Would you like to do me a favor, if possible?"

"Be happy to, if I can."

"A certain family employs me often to baby-sit, and they want me tomorrow night, but I want to take the long weekend for a trip south to the beach. You know, Monday the 14th is the big national holiday in France— 'liberté, egalité, fraternité!' Could you do it for me?"

Thoughts of possibly being with Ernst conflicted with desire to help her out, as I doubted she could find anyone else this particular weekend. I asked about details, and she explained. It seemed almost everyone in the dorm was leaving.

"I'll do it for you."

"Ah, a thousand thanks! You're a dear! They may want you Monday also. Not sure."

"That would be fine. I'm on the list, but this is my first opportunity. Maybe they'll recommend me to others, *if* I deserve it."

"But of course. I may even lose my job!" We smiled.

"I'm planning on a trip next weekend to Marseille to visit friends," I told her.

"Oh, lovely! Be sure and go east for a swim on the Riviera."

"We probably will, at some beach along there. I'm quite excited about it. Hope you have lots of fun on yours."

"We will! I'm glad your friend is doing well, and thank you again, Melanie. Better get back so I can pack. I told the family I'd try to get you, so I'll call them to confirm. Many thanks!"

" 'Night, Jeannie. Have fun and behave yourself."

Ernst called me at noon Friday, reported he was still hurting and a bit weak, but wanted to see me. Would I go to the pension to see him? I said yes, by taxi, knowing that would be his next request, and explained the details about my "new job" in the evening. Sounding reluctant, he said it would give him a chance for more rest and early bedtime. He also asked if I would be picked up and taken back, for the "job," and I assured him I would be. *Love you,* I thought.

"See you about two, room 207, then?"

Hesitating a second, I vowed good behavior to the Lord and said yes.

CHAPTER 14

A definite need to pray and be in the Scriptures pervaded me, and though hungry, I decided to fast in place of getting lunch. *Teach me the value and blessing You promised in fasting, Lord,* I prayed, *for I need Your wisdom and Your help today.* Much praise and prayer ascended as I meditated in the Word of God, and surprisingly, even my hunger decreased as help from Him was given.

At two o'clock I knocked three times softly on room 207 at the pension. Ernst opened it, and after I went in he explained that today he'd like to stay as scarce as possible from the tour group he'd be with for two weeks.

"Most of them are out seeing Paris now, but tonight is Henri's night off, and the group eats here tonight, so soon enough I'll have to take care of details and any difficulties. The fellow who took my place did a good job at de Gaulle and check-in today. He's an old friend, and you'll be interested to know that he's a Christian, Melanie."

"Really? How long have you known him?" I asked, sitting on a chair he indicated.

"Mm, long enough to have discussed religion. Would you believe he even mentioned Eurofest?"

"Wow, great! Is he going?"

"He wasn't sure, but he'd really like to." He sat down on the bed rather wearily.

"Are you all right?" He nodded dubiously. "You must take it easy as much as possible. We do have a lot to thank the Lord for, Ernst."

"Yes — if you look at it like that," he shrugged with a slight wince, either in pain, or as though tired of the subject, or both. "You were kind to help our friend Jeannie out tonight, Melanie."

"It was a bit of a decision, knowing I could have been with you. Hope you don't mind, Ernst. She'd surely never have found anyone else."

"Probably best," he said reluctantly, then paused. "I've been doing a lot of thinking, Melanie. Flat on my back for a change."

"God puts us there sometimes, they say, to show us things."

"You're a rarity, Mel! You and your personal God. Look, let me get something off my chest. You've been patience personified. He's best left nameless, to you, but the fellow I fought yesterday and who followed you was a former friend, or at least an accomplice."

"You don't have to tell me, Ernst." I said, dreading to hear about it.

"Well, let me say I've been on the fringe, more or less, of the radical movement on the continent, politically, if not completely in ideology. I'll spare you details, if you prefer, but I've been in pretty deep. Reason the bloody fools got after you was to get me to do more dirty work. They planned to kidnap you and blackmail me, knowing I couldn't very well go to the police."

"Oh, Ernst!" I shuddered at the whole mess, especially the thought of being held by those creeps. "They must have wanted you badly. How did you find out their intentions?"

He looked at me guardedly. "Ilse finally told me, after I took you back to your dorm Tuesday night. You see, she'd met me in London, apparently by chance, staged to look accidental, when my tour was over. I hadn't seen her for a long time. We flew back to Paris together Tuesday. It was her job to spy on me while they got you. But when you stumbled into my arms and described the scoundrel, I suspected a connection. You really did a masterful job of eluding him."

"Jesus helped me, Ernst. I sure had no possible idea I'd find you here! Wonder how the other fellow is. You said you didn't know him."

"I couldn't care less how he is. Almost never do we know more than one contact." He paused. "Melanie, there's more."

"Do you *have* to tell me?" I groaned, half wanting to hear, half not.

"You know what they say, 'Confession is good for the soul.'"

"But I'm not your priest!" For the first time, I realized something. "So that's what the doctrine of the priest-hood of all believers entails. Maybe I am." Not only intercessory prayer, praise and possibly fasting, but . . . confession too?

"You lost me." His mind was of course on a different track.

"Sorry, Ernst. Tell me, if you must."

"I've been dealing, Mel. Hash, mostly." His express-ive face revealed guilt, apology and penitence. "I never wanted you to know, but. . . . Smuggling dope on the coaches across the borders is serious enough, but I've been scared of getting in deeper for a long time, and decided to quit before you came. You know, don't you, what they wanted me to move?"

"Heroin?"

He nodded grimly.

Revulsion unsettled my stomach, and I looked away. If this didn't kill love, surely nothing could.

"No more, Melanie. I told them to get lost, and I'm out of it, for good. I'm terribly sorry for the trouble I've caused you. You'll have no more, but just for good measure, I've asked Henri to check on you a bit."

Thoughts tumbled. "Ilse? Is she still in all this too?"

"I did my best to persuade her to run while she still could. As far as I know, she did."

"I hope so." Another thought occurred to me. "Ernst, why did you decide to tell me all this when you were so determined not to before? Are you trying to get rid of guilt by doing so?"

He was silent. Then, "Possibly."

"Ernst, you'll never get rid of guilt except by turning to the Lord Jesus Christ, repenting and taking Him as your sin-bearer. That's the only way. He not only forgives, but He takes away guilt, cleanses and gives you a new heart! He makes you a whole new person!"

Beads of perspiration showed on his forehead and a look of pain crossed his face, but first I thought I had seen a tiny trace of . . . what? Hostility or hope? His hand moved toward his bandaged neck and shoulder as he grimaced.

"It hurts, doesn't it? Such a shame. Should we change the bandage?"

He nodded. "I've got what's needed, if you'd be so kind again. You're a good little nurse."

"No praise deserved, but glad to do it." I set to work, was fairly pleased with the progress of the wound as I prayed in the Spirit for the Lord's healing, body and soul.

The bandaging stopped more talk of spiritual matters, but we discussed the itinerary of his trip and our respective plans. He asked where Aunt Kate and I would be staying in Brussels, and told me he'd be seeing his family, for his tour group would spend two nights in Vienna. His tour would be over on my birthday, Saturday, the 26th.

After a while conversation lagged as Ernst seemed lost in thought. Finally he said, "Melanie, I may have given you a wrong idea as we've talked. You seem to have such a personal concept of God — as you've described it, an actual relationship. My concept is totally different. In fact, if you knew it, you'd probably consider me atheistic. To me, 'God' is an idea. Your concept of 'God' I consider simply auto-suggestion, as a psychologist would term it. To me, 'God' is freedom; to be my own boss, run my life, unhampered by demands of others, with no fear of death, which is negated. It's a negation of the meaningless existence we call life, and so 'death' is conquered, in a sense. So is 'life,' as we term it. I call it corrupt, society talking about a 'God' who evidently doesn't exist. Before now, I never felt like discussing this with you. Have you ever studied Schopenhauer or Hermann Hesse?"

"Yes, superficially, but I've found an infinitely better way . . . ."

"See, man being his own boss, fully controlling his environment, can in his own way strive for a utopia. Hence my interest in architecture — to help beautify the world."

"In modern terms, Ernst, it seems to me you're doing just as the ancient Israelites did. 'Every man did that which was right in his own eyes.' It leads to humanism, and the result *then* was chaos, as it will be in our world before long, if your view continues to hold. I love beauty too, but—"

"You know, Jim Harding said something yesterday about a theology of humanism which he's convinced will develop, finally, into worship of a world leader he called 'Man of Sin,' or Anti-Christ. It was interesting, all about a detailed future program of events, culminating in an actual physical return of Jesus Christ from Heaven! Fantastic! I never heard of such a thing, and he says it's all in the Bible."

"He's absolutely right, Ernst. And when Christ comes and defeats the forces of evil led by Anti-Christ, as I understand it, He'll set up a perfect society for the first time in history. It will be perfect because it will be a theocracy ruled by Jesus Christ, who is God. To me, it's thrilling! And He can come at any time. We're to be ready at all times for His coming."

"Jim said the same. Something about 'times of the Gentiles.' Quite involved but interesting."

"Ernst, this 'negation of life and death' — how do you square this with actual physical death?"

"Death is simply cessation of existence, not to be concerned about. I'm free from all hangups most people contend with."

"But then I came along and upset your 'freedom.' "

He grinned. "Yes, you did! And you had to become a zealot; I hadn't counted on that!" Then his smile became tender. "You offered me real love, and gave me a measure of it."

"A measure, with limits, but God offers you love without limit. And perfect freedom, and *life*. Jesus said, 'If the Son shall make you free, you shall be free indeed.' And 'He that believeth on the Son hath life, and he that believeth not the Son shall not see life, but the wrath of God abides on him.' Ernst, He's more real and precious than anything or anyone I've ever known, believe me!"

"You're beautiful, Melanie, especially when you get that certain look in your blue eyes."

"What look?"

"I don't know. You have something beautiful indeed."

"I have Jesus. He makes even the ugliest beautiful, praise Him."

He got up, bent over and gently kissed my forehead and said, "Let's go for a stroll. We need some fresh air."

"Love to." It was rather warm in the room.

The light breeze outside was refreshing, as we walked over to the canopied sidewalk market across from the metro station as we had done the day of my arrival. The same thought came to us both, for he expressed my exact thought, "A lot has happened since our first day together."

I thought with a shiver how different this market was in daylight from what it was at night.

As before, we bought some fruit and ate it as we walked. He said he'd arranged for me to eat with the tour group at the pension, if I liked, and I found I could fit it in before time to be picked up at my dorm for the baby-sitting. Then we headed back, for their bus had pulled in.

It was interesting studying the group he'd be with on his tour, and I felt strangely self-conscious as we sat together later at a small table in the dining room. I commented with a twinkle, "I'd better make sure there aren't any pretty chicks here with a birthday in the next two weeks!"

He laughed. "Hm. I'll take a good look and let you know. Later!"

When my taxi came, he opened the door, saying, "I'll see you tomorrow as planned, chérie. Good luck tonight."

I got in, turned and said, "Take care of that shoulder, and get lots of sleep tonight." He kissed his finger tips to me in the French manner as he closed the door. However, as he turned away, I thought he looked tired, pained and quite unhappy.

CHAPER 15

The baby-sitting went smoothly. The baby girl was already asleep when I arrived, and there were two little boys, who played until bedtime and finally quieted down after I read to them and told them a couple of Bible stories. Later, sometime after midnight, after asking me to sit again for them Monday night, their father very politely saw me to my dorm door for which I thanked him. I noticed with relief that at least a few other girls and fellows had stayed in the dorm over the weekend.

Saturday I slept very late, awakening with an almost drugged feeling, probably from all the week's pressure and a repressed nervousness about being in the almost empty dorm. Later I went for the mail and found letters from Mother, Dad, and Johnny all in one envelope. It was grand hearing from Johnny, who told me to say hello to Ernst for him. Mother wrote much welcome news about her new joy in the Lord Jesus, and Dad seemed jollier than ever.

The burden of postponed action regarding separation from Ernst lay heavily on me, and again I decided to fast and meditate in the Scriptures. I spent a blessed hour with the Lord. Somehow I felt that this weekend was crucial; that when we parted Sunday, I should let him know my decision, once for all. Meanwhile the Lord gave me a peace about just leaving it in His hands for now and going on as before, with the assurance of His presence and power.

As we'd arranged, Ernst picked me up at the dorm early Saturday afternoon. We decided to take in the Matisse collection at the Museum of Modern Art, which we'd missed before, and we both enjoyed it. Then we saw a marionette show in the Bois de Boulogne and strolled through the lovely gardens there. Again we ate dinner at the pension with his tour group, after I had again changed his bandage in his room, quite pleased with the healing of the cut.

As we approached my dorm in the evening, I remarked, "I had the eeriest feeling both last night and tonight in the dining room that I was being watched."

"Perfectly natural, for such a pretty girl as you." His tone somewhat reassured me.

"I'm glad you seem to be feeling so much better, Ernst. Hope you don't have any trouble with the cut on the tour."

"Same here. I should be doing better from now on. See you tomorrow, bright and early for church, right here?"

"I'll be ready, and looking forward to it, mon chéri," I said, pushing my hair back.

He reached out and drew me to him, searching my eyes, then bent and kissed my lips softly, tenderly. It went all through me, and we stood there in embrace, enjoying the moment's deep pleasure.

"Bonne nuit, chérie," he whispered, then turned abruptly and walked away as I entered the door.

"Take care," I called back as he turned, nodded and waved. But I thought weakly, how can I lose you forever?

Sunday morning we rode a rather deserted metro, arriving early at the little church. In the worship service,

Laurie sang her best yet with "The Good Shepherd" by Beardsley Van de Water, a powerful and moving rendition of the Twenty-third Psalm.

"Magnificent voice," Ernst whispered to me, and I nodded.

Just before the sermon, Jim explained that by request from several, he and his wife would sing a duet. My eyes misted as I listened, realizing how much this couple meant to me, though such recently made friends.

The sermon was a deep blessing. Based on the first chapter of Colossians, it was a lucid and logical presentation of the Person and redemptive work of Jesus Christ, the "image of the invisible God, the firstborn of every creature, by whom all things were created, in Heaven and earth, visible and invisible. . . ." Powerfully Jim proclaimed how this One, Jesus Christ, holds together all things by the word of His power, and is the Head of God's body, the church universal, possessing in all things preeminence by virtue of having, through the blood of His cross, reconciled all things to Himself.

Clearly he presented the absolute authority of the Scriptures as evidenced by fulfilled prophecy within them, Christ's resurrection, the presence of Israel in the world, and the completely changed lives of those who have believed in the revealed facts and doctrines of the Word of God. Poignantly he appealed to us who once were "alienated and enemies in our minds by wicked works, now reconciled, to continue in the faith grounded and settled, and not be moved away from the hope of the gospel." He defined "the hope of the gospel" as the assurance of eternal salvation given to those who believe, based on the nature and promise of a holy God, the Father of our Lord Jesus Christ.

The thrilling climax of the whole was the revelation of

the "mystery" hidden from past ages, which is "Christ in you, the hope, or assurance, of glory."

Following the sermon, Jim gave a loving and moving appeal for any who wanted Jesus to enter their lives, to come to the front so he could pray with them. I could almost feel a tension in Ernst, and glancing at him I saw beads of perspiration on his forehead, his mouth a firm line. I closed my eyes and prayed that the evil one would be cast away and God's power be manifested. Though I wanted to ask him if he wished to go forward, something held me back, and the closing hymn was announced. The moment had passed, though Jim held the invitation open until the last verse.

After the service, Marg appeared and hugged me in welcome, then told Ernst, "I'm glad you came too!" He smiled at her, then David and several others greeted us warmly. The Debards again invited us to dinner, but we had decided to eat in town, as Ernst had to meet those in his tour group who wanted to go out to Versailles for the afternoon. We thanked them just the same.

At the door, Jim and Laurie beside him greeted us cheerily.

"Your solo, Laurie, and your duet were both lovely, and thank you for the superb sermon," I told them.

Ernst added, "Yes indeed, it was a good service."

They nodded in thanks and Jim said, "All praise to Him. We're really glad you came with Melanie, Ernst. Oh, David has a couple of books I promised you. He's here somewhere."

Marg, still with us, said, "I'll get them," and dashed off, returning in a couple of minutes with Stuart Briscoe's *Living Dangerously,* Kenneth Taylor's pamphlet, "Is Christianity Credible?" and C.S. Lewis' *Mere Christianity.*

"A small potpourri of literature, as you expressed an interest," Jim smiled.

"Thanks. I'll return them."

"No problem."

Laurie told me she'd meet my train in Marseille, Friday, and to let them know in case of any change of plans. So we parted, not without a tinge of unspoken regret.

"Keep trusting," she whispered in my ear, as we hugged each other. Marg was the last one who waved to us, as we walked away from the church.

I decided I'd like to see Versailles again, so after lunch we met and accompanied those of the group who were going, using the chartered motor coach they would be traveling in for the tour starting the next morning.

We sat in the front seat together, and when Ernst identified landmarks over the loudspeaker every so often, I relived part of the thrill of my first tour of Europe a year ago. Listening to him brought it all back. Underlying and dispelling the thrill, however, was a heaviness of spirit, a nagging disappointment over his lack of response at church in the morning. My hopes had been so high.

He turned and winked at me. "You look wistful. Having fun? See how it could be?"

I knew what he meant, smiled a bit and nodded.

The coach driver, a jovial Dutchman to whom Ernst had introduced me, glanced over at us, grinned and began singing the words of a current hit song, "I love you, I honestly love you . . . ."

My eyes twinkled, for it seemed to be our theme song for the summer.

"Now, now, Hans," Ernst said to him. "Just wait."

I remembered the joshing he'd had with our driver last year, and my mood lifted as I glanced around behind us at the smiles of the other passengers. The eerie feeling of being watched returned, however.

Again awed at the magnificence of the palace and exquisite gardens, we kept up the lightheartedness of the occasion pretty well, enjoying each other and exclaiming over the beauty of it all. Yet beneath it, a heavy feeling of our impending separation kept lowering my spirit, for I not only hated partings, but this parting could be our last. Should it be, I asked myself, wondering how I could possibly call it quits between us.

Somehow he managed to keep me fairly high with laughs and fun all afternoon and evening, especially as it was the eve of France's Independence Day, and mobs were out celebrating. As we finally approached my dorm hand in hand, nothing had yet been said either of the morning service or of separation of any kind.

It was only at parting that he said, "Melanie, never in my life have I been so deeply affected as I was in that service this morning."

I couldn't speak, afraid I'd lose emotional control. I just gazed up at him weakly, moved my hand tentatively up his uninjured side to his face in a soft caress, and he pulled me against him and kissed me lingeringly.

Then he whispered in my ear, "I don't ever want to lose you, Melanie. I honestly love you."

His sweet words divided my heart and spirit asunder.

CHAPTER 16

In that way we parted. I could not do otherwise; I could not bring myself to break it off. Was not the future, after all, in God's hands, and had He not told me to leave it there? Was not my entire life in His hands? My weakness was too much to control.

No matter this man's past, and even his present state of being, I loved him. Some of his past activities, even if they were to cease as he'd avowed, I shrank from in distaste, but who was I to stand in judgment? Retribution was God's business, not mine. In spite of everything, I'd sensed a depth of character, a potential, in him that I'd never seen in any other fellow. He could be so tender and understanding, though I'd seen him harassed, annoyed, brusque and even ill-mannered on our tour a year ago, and somewhat so more recently. But so earnestly had I prayed for him. . . . Surely love is never in vain, nor prayers, I mused that night just before a fitful sleep came.

The persistent ringing of the hall telephone woke me up Monday morning. Sleepily I thought, I should answer it, as I glanced at my clock and saw it was almost eleven. July 14th, France's Independence Day, no classes, but within I recalled a vague fear that I'd better stay close to the school. I half stumbled out to the phone and picked up the receiver.

"Hello? Melanie Alexander speaking."

"Ah, happy 14th!" I heard. "This is Henri Bonnard."

"Oh! Henri. How are you?"

"I'm sorry if I woke you up."

"No problem. About time I was up."

"I have some free time today. Would you like to have lunch and see the big parade with me?"

Collecting my jumbled thoughts, I said, "Sounds good, yes. When?"

"I'll pick you up at your dorm in . . . an hour?"

"Fine. I'll be downstairs. A bientôt."

Noon saw us joining all the noisy, gay Parisians celebrating the big day. We ate lunch at a packed sidewalk café on the Champs Elysées, then joined the thickening crowds as we crossed the Place de la Concorde and followed the parade down the Rue de Rivoli. Such a hilarious populace, I thought, catching their enthusiasm and glad for Henri's companionship. He proved good balm for what might have been a lonely day. We laughed and clowned, shoved along with the multitudes enjoying the city's extravaganza on parade as it proceeded toward the Place de la Bastille. The stirring strains of the *Marseillaise* still rang in our ears as we finally veered off to stop at a café for drinks.

"You're fun, Henri!" I said to him in French, sipping a Coke. "So glad you called me."

He leaned forward, his twinkling hazel eyes full on me, and said, "It's indeed the greatest of pleasure being with you, Melanie." His hand lay halfway toward me across the small table.

Oh, the inimitable charm of the French, I thought, smiling as I pushed my hair back. "Thank you, Henri."

"Your accent becomes almost perfect Parisian."

"I'll hug you for that!"

He chuckled. "I hear you plan on a visit to Marseille this weekend, yes?"

I nodded and told him of my plans to visit the Hardings, explaining who they were.

"I was planning on a weekend at the Riviera myself. Would you be interested in driving down as far as Marseille in my car with me?"

Surprised, I asked, "*Really*, Henri? You're not just — you're sure?" He nodded, and I exclaimed, "How sweet of you! Didn't even know you had a car. Are you going with anyone else?"

"I plan to meet friends there. I'd be most happy to take you down and bring you back too, if we can schedule times."

Delighted, I agreed, and we worked out both schedules and plans.

After some more fun around town, he left me at the dorm later in the afternoon, as I had some reading to do and a baby-sitting job that evening.

"Till Friday, then, looking forward to it. Have a good week."

"You too, Henri. It was grand fun. See you then."

Classes, projects and a couple more baby-sitting jobs took up most of my time during the week. Jeannie came and regaled me with tales of her weekend, and we got better acquainted. It was a relief having the dorm more occupied again.

To my joy, Ernst called Tuesday and Thursday nights, and I told him of our plans for the weekend, which he seemed to approve, though on the second call he sounded very solicitous for our safety. He said his shoulder was healing fairly well. It was so good to hear his voice, in spite of his strange anxiety.

Thursday I received a letter from Aunt Kate with final details for our trip worked out. She had decided to fly directly to Brussels and meet me at our hotel there.

Early Friday Henri came for me, and we were soon traveling south in his gleaming little tan Fiat. He complimented me on my "chic" outfit I'd splurged on in a Paris shop, and I admired the way his blond hair and light complexion matched his cool summer sport togs.

"Like your car. Do you ever drive to work?" I asked. Like a Parisian, he drove fast but skillfully.

"Sometimes, but I go mostly by metro. Petrol's out of sight, so it's better to go that way."

"Good to be out on the open road again. Been cooped up in Paris pretty long. Never thought I'd say that, though."

He smiled as he glanced over at me. "Hope you've enjoyed our city."

"Oh, I *love* Paris! To think over half my time here is gone makes me a little sad. Glad I have a few more weeks, anyhow. So far I haven't been a bit homesick."

I told him about Eurofest, to begin in Brussels the next week, and my plans to drive up with the Hardings. He seemed quite interested in the plans and purpose of it, to instruct and teach youth in the Scriptures, give them training in discipleship, and in how to witness to their faith in Christ in all the countries they represent.

"Just what I very much need," I commented. "Have you read much in your New Testament?"

With a guilty look, he answered, "A little, but not as much as I should."

"Wish you could go with us. I wish Ernst could go," I sighed wistfully.

He glanced at me quizzically. "You're quite different from Ernst. I'm a little surprised you two hit it off so well."

I wasn't sure exactly what he meant. "Different?"

"Well, you seem so settled and satisfied with your faith, and Ernst is . . . well, definitely not religious!" The emphasis on his words made me uncomfortable. I decided to probe some.

"You probably know much more about Ernst than I do. What do you think of him?"

"He's 'cool,' as they say, and I like him. Ernst is a rather intense person. Likes to try his hand at every challenge, and does it well. Not satisfied with mediocrity."

"Hm, yes. Go on." I was most interested.

"All the same, he can be impatient, and at times quite intolerant. I think he has the Austrians' sense of superiority, a quality we French often exhibit too."

"You must, indeed, know him well. He's told me of some of his past activities."

His searching glance appeared knowing and cautious. "Oh?" I suddenly wanted to change the subject, feeling it unfair to Ernst, when his next words set me back. "Yes, I know all about them."

Not wanting to hear more, I said, "I'm trying to forget all that, and I've been praying for his salvation, Henri. Remember what I told you about the new birth?"

He nodded and said, "That's a big order, Melanie. You must have a great faith."

"The Lord is a great God, Henri."

As we drove steadily and made good time on the new superhighway, I enjoyed the French countryside, with its many grape arbors and pretty patchwork cultivation. We stopped for lunch near Baune, by-passing Dijon.

While we ate, he described in glowing terms the surpassing beauty of the Côte d'Azur on the drive east between Marseille and Cannes — the French Riviera on the blue Mediterranean.

"The drive, named the Grande Corniche, is recognized as one of the most scenic highways in the world," he explained. "I'd love to show it to you."

"I'd love to see it."

"We couldn't get there before dark, even if we by-pass Marseille, but it's lovely by night too. We could drive to Cannes, stay over, and return to see its loveliness by morning light. Would you like that, Melanie?"

I began to perceive his possible meaning. Even so, the proposal was tempting, certainly not the first made to me, nor the first I'd resisted or fallen to. "It's very tempting, but the Hardings are expecting me tonight, Henri."

"There are telephones! You'd have a chance to see fashionable St. Tropez, the famous Cannes, perhaps Nice, too. . . . They'd understand, surely."

Too well, I was afraid. I'd phoned during the week to tell them we'd be driving instead of my taking the train. "Where are you meeting your friends, Henri?" *Was* he meeting friends?

"At Cannes, but it can be postponed till tomorrow after I take you back to Marseille."

Harmless, perhaps, but. . . . They say the Frenchman always tries, I thought with irony, though it struck me, as such a good friend of Ernst's, strange that he would. Was he testing me? The question supplied the decision.

"No, thank you, Henri, we'd best keep our plans intact. I do appreciate your taking me all this way, to the Hardings.'" Gently touching his wrist as it rested on the table, I looked straight into his eyes. There was regret, then resignation in them, but no more was said, and we were soon on the road again.

We followed the picturesque Rhone River Valley south, by-passing Lyon and Valence, and ate supper in charming Avignon. It was almost nine o'clock when we pulled up at the apartment complex in East Marseille where the Hardings lived.

"You're an excellent driver, Henri, and equally good at following directions in city traffic. You must be tired, and you need a break. Come on and meet my friends."

He agreed, and with more jotted directions given me by Laurie, we found their apartment and were warmly welcomed by the family, except for David who was out with friends. Marg, dressed for bedtime, hugged me and stayed up only long enough to help serve us all cool drinks and some cookies. As soon as she went off to bed, Henri said he had some way to go yet and stood up to leave.

"I'll see you about two o'clock Sunday afternoon, Melanie. Au revoir, all of you, and thank you for the delicious punch and cookies," were his parting words.

"Many thanks, Henri. Have a good time."

Perhaps it was premonition, but a strange anxiety nagged me as I watched him go.

CHAPTER 17

Laurie, Jim and I talked for some time after he left, then David came in with a warm "Welcome to Marseille! All set to take in the big town?"

"Hi, David. Sure am. You look real good. Pardon my Virginia slang."

"I remember," Jim chuckled, running his fingers through his hair as David grinned. "Takes me back. Melanie, we thought you might enjoy seeing the Mission headquarters in the morning, then after lunch drive east along the Grande Corniche on the famous Côte d'Azur and stop for a swim in the blue Mediterranean."

"Sounds simply divine," I said, feeling rewarded for resisting the temptation of seeing it with Henri.

"You may also like to see the Chateau d'If, where the Count of Monte Cristo was imprisoned," Laurie added, to which I nodded vigorously. "But I'm sure you're tired after all day on the road, so let's see about your room."

Their three bedroom apartment was tastefully furnished, and I found that I had a twin bed in Marg's room which doubled as a guest room. I gave Laurie a hostess gift of linens from Paris and told her that the next day I'd give Marg and David some candy I'd brought for them. When I'd prayed and retired, the bed was so comfortable that I'm sure I was out in minutes.

All but Laurie went with us in the morning, and Jim's explanation and demonstration of the North Africa Mission's work fascinated me. He introduced me to the mission "family," who all were most friendly and welcomed me warmly. Then we drove west across town and took the launch out to the very picturesque Chateau d'If Island. Exploring the high-cliffed isle was an adventure for me, a fun time for all of us, and I took some pictures with my little camera.

After lunch at the apartment, we all dressed casually for the beach, took a little friend of Marg's named Becky, and leaving the busy metropolis behind we approached the coast. The drive became lovelier and more scenic the closer we got to the violet-hued mountains, or "hills," as David said. The view of the majestic Notre Dame de la Garde Cathedral high on the hill overlooking Marseille vaguely recalled castles on the Rhine in Germany, and rivaled Sacré Coeur Basilica in Paris. I fell in love with the exquisite Côte d'Azur.

We drove beyond Toulon to St. Tropez, stopped for some refreshing ice cream, then back to a most inviting beach.

"Yes, the Mediterranean is incredibly blue, out beyond the area of lovely limpid green hue," was my comment as I prepared for the tempting water, then raced David and the girls for the first dip in the breakers. Laurie and Jim followed more slowly. It was more than worth the long drive the day before and the day to come, I thought with intense joy.

Later we sunbathed on the sand, and it felt so good to relax completely again.

"I feel like I've been wound up tight as the string in a baseball, and I'm loosening up," I told Laurie as we watched Jim, David and the girls jumping and riding the

144

waves. "This is so marvelous! Why have you all been so super to me, Laurie?"

She studied me a few seconds, then said, "You're a very sweet Christian girl, Melanie, and we love you, but you know, I confess there's another reason."

"Oh? Tell me."

"Well, you remind us of someone. Both Jim and I felt the same way, and it's a bit of a story." She paused. "Five years ago in May, the Lord gave us a third child, a darling little girl."

"Really?"

She looked away sadly, I saw. "She — she lived only three months."

"Oh, what a . . . how you must have suffered." My throat tightened with compassion as she nodded.

"Shortly after she was born, the daughter of friends— a girl about your age, though not as pretty as you — came over from the States to stay with us for the summer and help with the baby. Though her parents are Christians, she was rebellious, didn't want any part of it. She was enchanted with the stage and wanted to make it a career. Her parents were opposed, and offered her a trip over here to help us just when we had needed and prayed for someone. It had been a hard pregnancy for me. Well, to keep it brief, she came over, fell in love with little Amy Lee, and when the baby died, Carol was completely broken up — as were we at first." She paused, gazing sadly out across the Mediterranean. "Well, she finally yielded her life to Jesus Christ, went home, trained in Bible school and is now in North Africa as a young missionary. Little Amy Lee performed her ministry."

Her voice caught a little, and my eyes stung. "How precious, but how you must have suffered."

"Yes . . . Melanie," she spoke earnestly. "As a girl, I had everything. An only child of very wealthy parents, I was denied nothing. You have no idea how the Lord has had to deal with me, time after time, to bring me to Himself, make me dependent upon Himself alone. I couldn't wish the trials on you, but the rewards have been immeasurable. Well, you reminded us of Carol, somehow," she smiled. "And I doubt if you realized I'm carrying another child now, fourth month."

Amazed, I cried, "Are you, truly? Congratulations! I wouldn't have guessed."

Her smile increased. "This one is the Lord's extra-special gift, for I'm getting on in age. Probably the last one. We think it'll be a boy, but whichever, God is going to bless us all."

"I'll certainly pray and praise Him for that. And, thank you again, for telling me, and for your kindness. I'm glad I reminded you of Carol, though I couldn't measure up to that."

"Melanie!" Marg and Becky were running toward us. "Come help us build a sand castle! You too, Mama!"

I saw a look of irritation on Laurie's face at Marg's interruption, but she grinned at me with a shrug and we joined them, helped build a masterpiece which was pronounced "fair to middlin' " by Jim, with a wink at me. Then I took another swim. David and I raced each other beyond the breakers, and he beat me consistently with his long strokes. His love of the water was obvious.

The day was superb in every way, finished in the evening at "home" by family devotions with intercessory prayer for many, including Ernst, my parents, Johnny and Henri.

The crowning touch was a call from Ernst. Sounding very anxious, however, he asked if everything was all right, about which I left no doubt. He said they had arrived in Vienna that evening, and he was calling from home. His shoulder was much better.

"Mel...." A long silence.

"Yes?"

"Mel, I—"

"Ernst, are you...? What's wrong?"

Another silence, then, "Nothing. Please take care, Mel. Je t'aime."

The phone clicked as I murmured, "Je t'aime aussi," but a strange worry possessed me through a restless night.

Sunday morning we all attended their little French church and saw many of the missionaries I'd met the day before. They included Beverly and Paul McCullough and their family, who were partially supported by my church in Richmond, and who had just returned from furlough in the States by ship. Still, however, the memory of Ernst's call kept bothering me. Why had he sounded so troubled?

Marg sat on one side of me and David on the other, next to his parents. He was already quite a bit taller than I, and was attentive as he held the hymnbook for the three of us and looked down at me now and then during the sermon. A fine boy, I thought.

On the way home from church in the car, I asked him, "Have you decided yet what you're interested in doing when you finish school, David?"

With not a second's hesitation he answered, "I'd like to go into mission work, probably in North Africa, and if so, Algeria, where Dad was brought up, if it's still open by then. Sort of like to carry on the family tradition, you know." He grinned self-consciously.

"Great! Praise the Lord," I said.

"Most likely go to the States for college. Hope it'll be Wheaton."

"With his grades, there'll be no problem there," Jim put in from the driver's seat. "David's an excellent student."

"Like his father and grandfather," Laurie said.

"And his mother," Jim added with a loving smile at Laurie.

What an incredible family, I thought.

After another delicious meal I finished packing, took a few pictures of the family, and awaited Henri, who came very shortly after two o'clock.

"We'll see you at your dorm about eight o'clock Friday morning, Lord willing," Jim told me in farewell when I'd again thanked them all.

"I'll be ready. A bientôt!"

"Au revoir!"

Henri seemed in a hurry as he carried my suitcase and quickly laid it in the trunk of his car, after opening and closing the door for me.

"We have a long trip ahead, and it may be one o'clock in the morning before we get to Paris, *if* we make good time," he said, looking all around us as he revved the motor for a fast start.

He seemed nervous as he took chances in the city traffic, but seemed to know the way and drove expertly. I hooked my seat belt and kept conversation at a minimum till we were out of the city.

"Hope you had a good time," he said through tight lips and only the trace of a smile as he increased speed and glanced twice in the rear view mirror.

"Oh yes, super!" I told him all about my weekend, though he seemed rather preoccupied, kept looking in both rear view mirrors, and drove at a pretty risky speed. "Did you enjoy yours?"

"Yes, somewhat. Got a swim in, too, with friends, and ran into some acquaintances." Noncommittal, he offered little more, and our chit-chat lessened as I became more concerned at his obvious tension. Something was wrong.

"Henri, you seem nervous and tense. Is something bothering you?"

He seemed to hesitate, then answered, "Forgive me for driving so fast, Melanie, but don't let it bother you, please."

Maintaining his speed, though, he kept moving his eyes from the road to the mirrors. I recalled with dismay that the average speed on this highway was 130 kilometers, or 81 miles an hour, and we covered the miles along the Rhone Valley with small talk at a minimum, for we were far over 130.

What on earth is the matter with him, I kept wondering. As though pursued. . . . Could it be? I glanced out the rear window and saw only one car a long distance behind us. But if so, by whom? And why? No, he's just in a hurry to get home, or to get me back. A few minutes later, I glanced back again. Same car, but it seemed to be closer. I noticed Henri had increased his speed. No others had passed us, and I kept noticing the same car about the same distance behind us, thanks only to Henri's speed. What's with all this? Is Henri involved in some caper? This is ridiculous, I thought, alarmed by now.

"Henri," I demanded, "are we being escorted or tailed?"

He growled, "I wish it *were* an escort."

"Then we are! What's the deal, and how long do you intend to keep me in ignorance?"

"I thought there wouldn't be need to tell you, my friend. Looks like I can't shake them, as I'd hoped. Wasn't even sure they'd find us."

"Who in the world are 'they'?"

"Strangely enough, I don't really know," he said with a tone of disgust.

"Are you —? What kind of an answer—? *Why* are they tailing *us?*"

"Frankly, I'd rather not say, Melanie."

"Oh, you're the limit! You're as bad as Ernst." Suddenly I started to grab his arm, barely restraining myself. "Henri, does this have anything to do with Ernst? Is he in some kind of trouble? *Please* tell me, if you know!"

"It looks like I'll have to, or die unforgiven. Someone informed me last night that Ernst may be in bad trouble. But I just don't know what these guys behind us have in mind. Obviously they're after you, and they intend either to catch us, or wreck us!"

CHAPTER 18

My heart sank. This time "they" might not fail or be foiled. What a place to be, in a speeding car on an open road, pursued by another car, and no way of summoning help.

But Ernst! What now? "Henri, what about Ernst? Tell me!"

"Someone in his tour group is smuggling a big supply of H. Whether he's involved or not, I don't know, Melanie, but I do know that's why you and I are in danger."

I groaned in alarm, protest and frustration. "They couldn't get his help to smuggle the stuff on the coach, so apparently they went ahead and did it without him," I cried.

"How do you know that?"

"He told me they tried to get him to do it, and he refused to. Who told you about this, Henri?"

"Do you remember Ilse?" How could I forget Ilse? I nodded. "I ran into her last night, but apparently it wasn't coincidence, for she tipped me off and said we may be in danger."

"*We?* Did she know *I* was in Marseille?" I asked.

"Not until I told her. She thought you were in Paris, and said they might try to get you there; then I told her.

She seemed to believe him innocent too, for she said with you in their hands they could control Ernst better at the borders, or if it was found."

Familiar. "But how did *they* know I was in Marseille when Ilse didn't? Is she still involved with this ring? Ernst said she'd quit, or thought she had."

"I can't imagine how they knew, and apparently she is still involved, to a point at least. The fact that she ratted on them to me seems to show she's trying to protect Ernst, and you. It also could mean she may get in bad trouble."

"Yes, but ... oh Henri, I'm sorry I've involved you in all this." I looked out our rear window and saw the black car moving closer, but Henri kept maintaining the distance with increased speed.

He shrugged. "We're in it together now. You know something else? If we'd gone to Cannes together Friday night, since they obviously knew you were down here, they might have gotten you then somehow." Our eyes met briefly with pregnant meaning. *Thank You, Lord, doubly,* I prayed.

"Henri, I know Ernst wasn't in on this." He nodded. "What do you think Ernst would do if ... if I weren't in danger? I mean, if he knew I was absolutely safe?"

"I don't know, Melanie. There are too many angles, and I don't know his thinking."

"I wonder! Just last night we talked on the phone. Now I know why he sounded so nervous." Suddenly I wanted to pray, and told him, "While you drive, Henri, I'll pray." He glanced at me incredulously and shrugged.

I closed my eyes and began to pray, *Lord, help!* Then I thought, No, that's not the way He's taught me in His Word. "Rejoice *always.*" "In *everything* give thanks, for this is the will of God in Christ Jesus concerning you." Here I am, absolutely helpless, unable to do one thing but sit here as we try to keep ahead of that car. Henri's driving *too fast, Lord!* — but I can't drive for him or tell him how. I must allow him to be master at the wheel and trust myself to him. *Lord, we're both in Your hands! I'm Yours, and I yielded my day to You this morning, so You're in control. Thank You, Lord. Whatever You bring to us, I praise You for it. Be with Henri as he drives. Thy will be done, Lord.*

I opened my eyes and kept worshipping the Lord, my mind focused on Him instead of on our imminent danger. Glancing over at Henri, my eyes met his, and he smiled at me. "Merci," was all he said, and my spirit rejoiced.

A while later, his eyes still often on both mirrors, he said, "We'll soon need petrol, and we'd better put our heads together." We worked out a plan for the next station we came to, hoping it would be fairly crowded. "This may have to be our only stop, *if* we're lucky. Be prepared for anything, I warn you, and stay in the car and keep your door locked."

"Don't worry, Henri, it won't be luck. God is in control, and He'll protect us, I know."

He smiled tolerantly at me. "Wish I had your faith."

"You can, Henri. Give Him your life, and trust Him. He's faithful!"

Before long, signs indicated a station, and we exited, slowing only enough to make it.

"Hope they'll need petrol too; they should. Here we go. Pray for an open tank."

"I have. I confess, I've also asked Him to make them wait for one!"

To our relief, a number of cars and people were in evidence. As he quickly emerged and began gassing the car and paid the attendant in advance, I looked out the back window.

The car, a black Fiat, drew up to the tanks on our right, stopping beside us, and the occupant on the far side swiftly emerged to gas theirs.

Opening his door, the driver, vaguely familiar even with sunglasses, stepped out, only a few feet away from me. To my horror, I recognized him instantly as the man who had pursued me from Montmartre to our pension — the same port-wine stain and receding dark hair, but this time sans beard! He glanced at my tightly shut windows and locked door, then walked around the back of the car toward Henri, who was talking to the attendant.

"Henri!" I leaned over to our open driver's door and screamed at him, "Henri, get in the car!"

Instantly Henri turned and jumped back in the car, closed and locked his door, and the attendant recapped the tank as the man reached it. Seconds later Henri was dodging pedestrians and other cars with skillful speed as we took the exit back to the highway.

"Phew! That could have been close! Thank You, Lord Jesus," I breathed. Looking back, I saw the two men switch places, having apparently finished their transaction. "I was so afraid he'd do something to you. Do you know that man, Henri?"

"No, as far as I know, I never saw him before."

"That was the same man who chased me on the metro! I bet he had a gun to use on you."

Henri's face seemed ghostly, tension showing the beating pulse in his temples. "I'd make a fair guess you're right, and they'd planned to get us somehow with it. Help me with this seat belt."

Reaching over to snap his belt I glanced at the speedometer, and my panic mounted as I groaned at the speed.

"Just pray we make it," he said with tight lips, "and

while you're at it, Mel, pray the police will catch them. I told the attendant to notify them, and I hope he got their license number."

I looked out our rear, and saw them quite far in the distance behind us. "I guess there's no possibility of losing them by going another way?"

"Definitely not. This new North-South Auto Route is probably the best thing that's happened to my country in many years."

Thank You, Lord, I breathed, once again closing my eyes and trying to focus my mind on Him in worship and trust, though my heart was beating triple time.

"They're gaining on us, Mel." I looked back and saw he was right. "This car wasn't built for prolonged speed like this. Try to relax and slip down further in your seat if they get too close. And pray that nothing... just keep praying. If I ever survive this ...!"

I glanced at him. Bless your heart, I thought, loving compassion filling me. Then I continued praying silently, for I saw we were still above 140, faster than I'd ever dreamed of going.

Trying not to see landmarks as they seemed to fly by, I left him to concentrate on his dangerous task, not wanting to see behind us, and praying fervently. Eternities later I heard it faintly, in the distance behind us. "Is that a siren?"

"Think so. Let's hope they decide to stop *that* car. If they don't, they'll be after us instead, which won't help much, this far from Paris."

He drove like a madman, for the black Fiat was definitely closing in on us, the occupants apparently determined to drive us off the road, or whatever. *Dearest Lord Jesus, I'm finding it terribly hard to praise You right now! I'm afraid my 'thanks' are just words of panic. Help me, Jesus, help us, and thank You. . . .*

Henri ordered me to slip down in my seat and brace my feet squarely in front of me, so all I could do was hear the siren louder and louder behind us.

"They're passing them, and they're both only 90 or 100 yards behind us!" Then he exclaimed, "Thank God, they've pulled *them* over! They're slowing down, Mel. We're losing them!"

"Oh, thank You, thank You, my Lord," a huge sigh of relief escaped me, even though our speed hadn't lessened much.

"Yes, they've got them; but at best, the police can't press charges on them, except for speeding, simply on my word to the station attendant that they were after us."

"You mean they can still —?"

"Yes, I mean we can gain distance now between us, but that's about all. We can't slow down much, but the police back there will help us a lot. Maybe the rats won't catch up again, let's hope, but they won't give up."

Only then did I look back, but they were almost out of sight, and Henri was going about 130 now, still a dangerous speed. I slumped down again, only a bit more relaxed, and noticed clouds forming round us, as the sun, getting low, was obscured.

"We can thank God, too, that the weather so far has been in our favor."

He nodded, still glancing in the mirrors frequently. "Looks as though it won't stay that way very long." A few minutes later, he said, "What's that? Another siren?"

My heart sank, for I heard the unmistakable siren too. Watching out the rear, I reported seeing in the distance what Henri confirmed as a patrol car. Reducing his speed considerably, he let them approach, and soon enough we knew we were their aim.

"This is all we need," Henri groaned as he slowed and stopped the car on the shoulder behind them.

The driver ahead stayed in his seat, and two men emerged from the patrol car, one a gendarme, the other in plain clothes from the back seat. The latter came to Henri's window, held out his wallet and said, "D.S.T."

Henri's eyes widened, and I blurted out, "D.S.T.? What's that?"

"Direction de la Sécurité du Territoire. Equivalent to your F.B.I."

CHAPTER 19

"Traveling at a pretty fast clip, weren't you?" the D.S.T. man asked seriously. "Driver's license, please."

"Yes sir," Henri said, handing him what he requested. After glancing at it, he handed it to the gendarme, who examined it in turn.

"You're Henri Bonnard?" Henri affirmed it, and the man looked across at me. "And your name, mademoiselle?"

"Melanie Alexander, sir," I said, utterly mystified.

"Good. It is as hoped. I wish to tell you that you are safe now. Your pursuers will soon be placed behind bars, as part of a smuggling ring. The identities of some of the members have just today been turned in. We've been on the lookout for the necessary evidence supplied today, so a number of them have been apprehended already."

Henri looked at me in amazement, and I looked from him to the D.S.T. man to the gendarme, leaned back and just couldn't keep the tears from filling my eyes. I felt like a fool, but my feelings were beyond description: vast deep relief, gratitude, thanksgiving.

"Who, may I ask, turned them in?" Henri asked him.

"I can't give more information, but it was a fellow now in Vienna named Neubauer. He also informed the Direction that you two might be under pursuit today on this road, so we were alerted when a petrol attendant called in to the Lyon police about your pursuers."

"Oh, Ernst!" Two tears slid down my face.

"We saw them caught behind us just about in time to save our lives, sir."

"Yes. The patrols who did so now have them securely." He turned to the gendarme, who handed back Henri's license to him, saying, "Under the circumstances, I recommend clemency for this speeding offense." I thought I detected a tiny hint of sympathy behind his sunglasses.

The gendarme looked at both of us and said, "Yes, I'm happy that I'm not picking up the pieces of what could have been. You may proceed now, with a much more moderate speed, M. Bonnard."

"Thank you a thousand times, sirs," Henri said in a relieved tone, and I added my profuse thanks. As we drove off, I waved at them gratefully.

The rest of the trip "home" was increasingly cloudy, and finally, in the Paris environs, heavy rain fell, but it no longer mattered, we were so relieved and happy. We stopped at one of Henri's favorite bistros and ate a good supper, though it was after eleven by then.

"What mystifies me is how Ernst had the courage to turn them in," Henri mused. "He's been in on it himself for some time, though I don't think he's ever dealt H."

I didn't even try to figure it out. I just rejoiced, though my gratitude lessened somewhat when he said, "He may have to do time for his part, or pay a heavy fine."

When we reached the front of my dorm sometime after one o'clock, the rain had become a fine mist, and I was so exhausted that I almost forgot to thank him. When he put my suitcase down, though, I threw care to the skies, put my hands on his shoulders and kissed him.

"Merci, Melanie. You were amazingly calm. You're a fantastic girl."

"Oh, *no,* Henri! I was *scared,* but it was Jesus Christ who did it all!"

"Well, I'm happy we made it, and it's like this. Bonne nuit, mon amie."

When I finally dragged myself into my room, I saw an envelope on the floor, probably slipped under the door. It was a note from Jeannie, saying she hoped I had a "super" weekend, and that there had been three phone calls for me. Two were from Ernst in Vienna with a request to return his call up to one o'clock, the second made just about midnight. The other was an unidentified caller, who had asked for me Friday, and whom she had told I'd gone to Marseille for the weekend. "Hope it was all right to tell him," her note stated.

Who was that? I wondered. Could it possibly have been that creep who nearly finished us both? Likely so. I'd ask Jeannie for more details in the morning. Though I wanted desperately to do so, it was also too late to return Ernst's call, so very shortly I fell into an exhausted sleep.

Something was ringing, persistently. Finally it stopped, and I opened eyes drugged with sleep only enough to see it was light. Then I heard my name as several knocks sounded on my door.

"Melanie Alexander, telephone call from Vienna!"

"Be right there." I sat up quickly and noticed it was seven o'clock, then hurried out and answered, identifying myself.

"Glorious morning, chérie!"

"Ernst! Oh! *How are* you?"

"Happier than I've been in my whole life, Melanie. I've been up since four, waiting to call you, and the morning star shone brighter over Vienna and the world than I've ever seen. Thank our Lord with me, Melanie, for your safe return, for He's mine now, and I'm His!"

"Ernst, *what are you saying?* Do you mean—?"

"Yes, darling, early yesterday morning, after the most miserable week of my life, I gave in to Him, surrendered the whole bit, everything, to Jesus Christ!"

I'm sure my heart was swelling all over my insides. "Ernst, *Hallelujah!* Thank You, Lord Jesus, glory to God! Oh, I — I'm going to soar right out of this building in a minute! Tell me about — oh, I want to *see you!*"

"I want to see you, too, tell you much more, and hear all about your trip yesterday. Since I'm at home I can talk some, but I must return to the group very soon now. My company is letting me finish my tour, but only on a sort of probation. I don't know yet whether I'll be able to keep my job."

"Oh, I hope you can, Ernst. Go on, *please.*"

"Hope so too. Details of the case must come when I see you, but I'm free on bond now. The whole thing kept me in turmoil all week, mostly at the borders, and especially when I thought of your going to Marseille, even in Henri's car, as you told me Tuesday night."

"One of the two who chased us, Ernst, was the same one who followed me from Montmartre! It was *ghastly.*"

"They have him now, chérie. May God have mercy on him."

"Bless you. I haven't yet had the grace to pray for him like that."

"The judge probably won't show much mercy. Before I go on, tell me those 'ghastly' details of yesterday."

I told him all of it, and he expressed genuine sympathy and profuse apology. Then I said, "Now tell me as much as you can."

"All right. By the time we reached Vienna late Saturday afternoon I was in such agony. I couldn't stand it, not positive whether any heroin had been delivered or not. So help me, I began to pray, but it did no good at all. There was no peace, no response, nothing. I guess the prayer was simply selfish, or only remorse rather than repentance. . . . In the evening a local guide took the crowd on a tour, and I came home. My family said I looked terrible, and I couldn't tell them a thing. It was my burden. We talked for hours, but when everyone had retired, I took a long stroll. One by one I remembered the things you had told me, and what I'd read in two of the books you and Jim lent me, and in those first few chapters in St. John's Gospel you suggested I read. I knew then that the only answer was to turn it all over to Him, give Him my life, the whole bit. Then somehow I knew I'd probably have to give myself up, and it was a fight. But He won, and finally I prayed, 'Lord, take it all; take me, with all my sins and crimes. I believe that Jesus paid for them all on the cross. Do with me whatever You choose.' Melanie, it's incredible, but He did, for I was filled with the most profound peace I've ever known, and a great burden seemed lifted off my shoulders. I went back, took care of a certain job, then slept like a baby for two hours and woke up with the most marvelous sense of God's presence in me, which lasted all day, especially when I talked with certain other authorities. More about that after I see you. This morning, too, is *fantastisch!*"

"It's so glorious, Ernst, praise the Lord! I just can't express my joy, but I know just how you feel."

"I know you do, chérie. I'm so glad you shared it all with me, and I'm sorry I was so hard on you, so skeptical. When I told my parents and the girls last night, they thought I'd . . . how do you say . . . cracked up, so I know the challenge I have ahead of me. We'll talk more. I'm dying to see you. I'll call you again tonight. Better go now."

"How can I wait till I see you, Ernst? I'm so excited!"

"Melanie, I've thought a lot about it and I've decided to go to Eurofest. Placards about it are all over Europe. I'll meet you in Brussels on Saturday, darling."

"Oh, *marvelous!* I can hardly *believe* it. Wish it were Saturday right now."

"I'll let you know details later. Have a good day."

"God bless *you* today, and thank you for calling, Ernst."

"Je t'aime beaucoup—éternellement."

CHAPTER 20

I'm sure I didn't just walk to classes; I soared, all day, on wisps of fleecy white clouds, and surely my feet didn't touch ground. Rejoicing, praying, praising, I did things and went places automatically, seeing, yet not seeing people I knew. My joy was unspeakable and full of God's glory. I could hardly contain it.

Jeannie greeted me after class, and I told her everything, quite sure now that the caller had been the same man. I was able to pray for him and his two companions, one the accident victim, even though they were probably cursing both Ernst and me in jail somewhere.

I stayed in the heavenlies all week, and every night Ernst called me from a different city. My euphoria was limitless. I wrote letters home and to many friends, of course including the Hardings. I sketched and painted scenes, went shopping, sightseeing, many things I'd feared doing for so long. What freedom, quelle joie! The mail brought some birthday cards, for Saturday was my birthday, and I would see Ernst!

Thursday evening I was ready to leave for Eurofest, and after Ernst's call, and a brief one from Henri wishing me well, I retired fairly early, to get plenty of sleep for the next several days. My plan was to return to Paris alone by Tuesday for classes, and Aunt Kate would rejoin me after Eurofest was over the next weekend. Ernst's plans would, of course, depend on him. After that there would be only two more weeks of school, and I wished it were all over. Vaguely I wondered, what then?

The Hardings picked me up on schedule Friday morning, and our rejoicing was great as we drove north. Marg snuggled against me and chattered like a magpie for a while, as David acted amused with her, and snapped pictures of the scenery along the way. We three were in the back seat.

"Melanie," Jim said, "you've had some rough experiences because of Ernst. Have you asked yourself why God has allowed this?"

"No, I really haven't, yet I do know He delivered me — us — from danger both times, and perhaps other times too."

"Yes, and you thanked Him, as you wrote us, even in the time of real danger, which was excellent, and He was with you all the way, right?"

"He sure was!"

"Sometimes when we pray for and have a deep burden for someone, God allows us to partake of His sufferings for us, on behalf of that person. It's indeed a blessed experience, hard at the time, but when it's over we see how He led us and carried us through. In our weakness His strength shines forth."

"Yes, I see. I hadn't thought of it that way."

"It's a privilege to partake of the sufferings of Jesus Christ."

What a lesson, and at what cost they had learned it, I thought, and said so, as we talked of many things.

We arrived in the quite modern metropolis of Brussels shortly after stopping for lunch. I noted the smooth electric street cars and we drove around the

Grande Place with its gold-trimmed buildings, sidewalk cafés and shops, then we took a few minutes to see the famous Mannequin Pis fountain not far from the main square.

The houses fascinated me, set in rows, each built with a different color of brick, several stories high, with beveled façade and balcony. White trim around the roof of many set them off well. Though wishing I could catch them by sketch, I was content to use my little camera, and just gaze at all the rest. Marg and David were also taking pictures.

We drove around the complex which had been the site of the 1958 World's Fair, with the Atomium, enormous model of the atom, rising high in the air a short distance away. The complex, the Palais du Centenaire, consisted of several buildings surrounding lovely fountains and areas of grass with flowers of all colors. This was where Eurofest was already underway, hundreds of young people in evidence all over, standing or sitting around in groups in the sun of the clear, brisk and breezy day. Obviously the afternoon session had not begun.

Not far off to the southwest was Heysel Stadium where the Reverend Billy Graham would preach that evening at the evangelistic crusade accompanying Eurofest. We stopped to register in one of the complex buildings, with many others still registering.

In preliminary correspondence, Jim and Laurie had applied to be counselors for the stadium meetings in the French section, so they were to pick up their special badges and materials at seven o'clock in the counselors' room.

Walking back to the car, we noticed one small group of kids sitting on the grass facing an older man.

"That's Billy Graham talking with those young folk," Laurie told us.

"It's great seeing him again, isn't it, darling?" Jim asked Laurie with a special smile. "It's been a long time."

"New York City, summer of '57," she smiled back in turn as they paused for a brief kiss.

Soon we left to find our hotel not far away, where we were to meet Aunt Kate.

While Jim and David took care of the car and luggage, Laurie, Marg and I entered the hotel lobby and went straight to the desk.

"This is sure cool!" Marg exclaimed as she gazed around at the rather luxurious lobby. "I'm glad we can stay here two nights at least." Laurie had told me her father had sent extra funds so they could stay in a nice hotel, and they had been fortunate to secure rooms in the same one Aunt Kate had for us, but they had decided to stay there only two days. They had been invited by the Greater Europe Mission to stay for the remainder of Eurofest at their recently purchased new site for the Belgian Bible Institute at Heverlee near Louvain, twenty miles east of Brussels. There Marg would participate with the other missionary children in a Vacation Bible School conducted by some of the GEM missionaries.

Ernst had told me he would be staying with a friend in Brussels. Most of the E-F participants were living in dorms in the complex, having brought their own sleeping bags, and some were in camping sites nearby.

Just as we turned away from the desk, I heard my name and caught sight of Aunt Kate waving and approaching us. Someone was beside her, waving, grinning. . . .

"Johnny!" I screamed in utter surprise and delight, running to him with arms outstretched for a hug, ignoring all possible embarrassment on his part. "I had *no idea*—"

"Keep your cool, Sis, and thank Aunt Kate and Dad," my little brother said with a big smile.

"I turned to her and we embraced and kissed each other as she said, "Just had to bring Johnny along to even things up."

"Oh thank you, Aunt Kate, you precious dear. That was super of you, and both of you surprising me like this. Come, meet my friends."

Jim and David reappeared just in time for all the introductions.

"I'm so happy and excited, and I've got the most *glorious* news for you both!" I exclaimed. "Ernst has surrendered his life to Jesus Christ! *And he's coming here tomorrow!*"

"Oh Melanie, how marvelous! Praise the Lord." Aunt Kate hugged me all over again, murmuring, "Thank You, Lord Jesus."

Johnny grinned and said, "Ha, I'll have to see it to believe that. Old Ernst, a Christian?"

"That's right, you knew him from last year, too," Jim spoke up. "I'm sure we'll all want to see it."

"He's really been reading the Bible this week," I told them. "You wouldn't believe how excited he is about what he's read."

"You should see Mom, Mel. You'd hardly know her," Johnny said, and I just rejoiced completely. "Of course she and Dad sent you their love."

We quickly settled into our rooms and drove back to the complex, parked the car and entered the Palais du Centenaire for the afternoon seminars, according to our preference. Aunt Kate and I chose "Helping New Christians," Laurie, Jim and Marg decided on "The Christian Viewpoint on Social Problems," David went to "The Calling and Qualifications of a Minister," and Johnny chose "The Occult."

Thousands of young people in all modes of dress met in the huge auditorium of the Palais, in which the seminars were held. They were divided into numerous groups according to language and subject, and the hum of voices was surprisingly low. We sensed a spirit of reverence and expectancy of God's blessing as we joined the thousands sitting on thin cocoa-matting spread over the concrete floor.

Overall theme for E-F was "Together in Christ," and the theme for the day was "Developing a Life-Style," with definite emphasis on the security of the believer.

Many of the group leaders we found were graduates of the European Bible Institute in Lamorlaye, north of Paris, where I had first met the Hardings. Others of them represented the German and Belgian Bible Institutes. Many of the language groups met in different rooms all over the complex. Our leader directed us in a most interesting session.

About five-thirty, all over the huge hall as the thousands dispersed, we could see many little groups of two or three discussing or questioning the leaders, with open Bibles, finding meanings that were now relevant in a new way. It was fascinating, even to Johnny, whom we soon found with the Hardings.

Having a couple of hours before the eight o'clock "evangelization" service at Heysel Stadium, we ate dinner in one of the Palais dining halls with the other delegates. Everyone was so friendly, and the spirit so loving that we were all overwhelmed. Jim and Laurie had met friends and were eating with them, not far from us.

"It's like a bit of Heaven here below," Aunt Kate commented as we ate. "As you know, we got here late yesterday afternoon, and there were over seven thousand delegates at last night's preliminary meeting in the big hall we met in today. Billy Graham preached, and I'd say about fifty of them made first decisions for Christ. I met my friend from Washington, one of the fifty or sixty E-F leaders, last night, and he's to join me after the meeting tonight for the music program in the auditorium."

"Good. I'll have a chance to meet him, and Johnny and I can go over with the Hardings, if you like."

"No, we can all go together, dear. Things aren't at all that serious!"

We smiled, and I remarked, "Marg, Johnny and David are sure hitting it off well." The three were discussing some subject with animation as they ate. "I *can't wait* till tomorrow at 1:30 when I meet Ernst!"

We all went early to Heysel Stadium, five or six minutes' walk from the complex. Thousands of kids were crowding into the stadium, and we heard snatches of many languages as we proceeded around the tiered gravel stands. Jim and Laurie stopped to get their materials, and we went on to one of the two French sections where they were to be counselors, and held seats for them. The stands were divided up into different language sections, where the service would be translated from English and broadcast over two loudspeakers in each section into its language. Everyone would hear the English.

Many were praying silently for God's blessing as the service began, and it was a thrilling experience for me to be a part of this international gathering in His name. Rather large delegations had come from Greece, Egypt, the Orient, Australia and South America, as well as Europe, the States and Canada. Eight thousand Eurofest delegates plus the general public (including Mr. Firestone, the American Ambassader to Belgium, who was introduced with his twenty-eight guests) made a total of twelve thousand people. It was the largest attendance ever at an evangelistic meeting in Belgium. The music was superb, and Dr. Graham, whom I had seen before only on TV, preached a stirring sermon, after which well over two hundred people walked down onto the cinder track surrounding the grass-covered field to commit or re-commit their lives to Jesus Christ. In a way, I wanted to join them, but didn't.

"We'll never be the same again after this service," was Aunt Kate's comment, and we all nodded in agreement as we waited for her friend and Jim and Laurie to come from the field.

CHAPTER 21

"Happy Birthday, Melanie!" Aunt Kate wakened me saying. "Saturday, July 26, 1975. May God bless you, dear."

"Thank you, same to you, Aunt Kate," I answered, stifling a yawn. "My twenty-second. And *this is the day*... that the Lord hath made! We'll rejoice and be glad, praise Him!" I sat up, shook out my hair and hugged my knees in anticipation.

It didn't take us long to get ourselves together and share a short devotion and prayer before breakfast time. She gave me a small gift which when opened I found to be a bracelet made up of some tiny scenes of Brussels. "How charming! Thank you."

"Just a wee remembrance for the time and place, dear."

"You shouldn't have, in addition to all this, but I'm glad you did," I laughed as we left our room to meet Johnny and the Hardings to drive to the Palais for breakfast.

Birthday greetings met me along with other precious though small gifts, as we all rode in the car. The day was superb — deep blue sky, sunny and cool.

At the nine o'clock Bible Study in the Palais hall, Bishop Festo Kivengere from the Anglican Church in

Uganda, who along with Luis Palau from Argentina was a morning Bible Study speaker, taught on the day's theme, "Building the Relationship with God." Simultaneous translation into seven or eight languages made the message clear to all.

Bible study seminars on the theme followed at eleven o'clock. The whole company was divided into mini-groups of ten, each with a leader, in which we introduced ourselves and further studied what the Bible said about the theme subject. It was a personal contact where we felt a kinship and deep interest in those in our own group. Aunt Kate and I were in the same one, English speaking, while Johnny and the Hardings were in others of the hundreds of groups. The Lord was quietly answering many questions and meeting many needs.

Since it was the weekend, the schedule was different, and instead of afternoon seminars there was to be a skit at two o'clock in the Palais hall. Evangelization at Heysel Stadium would be at four, rather than in the evening, and a big international E-F-sponsored music festival at the Place Rogier downtown would follow dinner. I kept glancing at my watch, hardly able to suppress my excited anticipation of seeing Ernst.

We all had lunch together, though I could hardly down a bite. Johnny and David took turns with, "Ernst missed the plane," "He let the time get away from him, so he couldn't make it," and "He decided not to come." I wrinkled my nose at them in mock disgust.

While the others stayed at the Palais, Jim drove me back to the hotel.

"This is sweet of you, Jim. I'm so high in the clouds, I'd probably have gotten lost on my own!"

"That's for sure," he teased, reaching out his hand to give my arm a gentle squeeze. "I'll leave you here at the hotel entrance, so you can have your reunion, though I'd like to be a crystal in the chandelier. We'll see you later, Melanie. God bless you both."

"Thank you mille fois . . . and you too," I said, waving back as I floated in the entrance.

He was standing near the desk in the lobby, and when he saw me, his face sparkled like many gems as he came and lifted me right off my feet in an embrace I'll never forget as he murmured, "My precious love, my joy."

"Darling Ernst." Our lips met softly in sweet reunion.

Slipping his arm around my waist, he said, "Let's take a stroll down a shady lane to a certain park. But first, Happy Birthday! I have something here for you. Also something else, but that's for later."

Reaching into an inside pocket, he handed me a little package. Thanking him, I opened it and saw a stunning cameo set of necklace, earrings and broach. The settings all matched the ring he'd given me almost one year ago, and I was entranced.

"Purchased at the same place near Tivoli Gardens, Rome."

"Oh, *thank* you, darling. I *love* them." Looking up at him, I added fondly. "And I love the giver of them."

"I love the One who brought you to me, and His gift."

His whole countenance was suffused with a glow that amazed me.

"You look so *different,* Ernst! Your face is . . .," I shook my head, seeking description, "almost beautiful."

"It's Jesus, Melanie! Don't you know? He's in me now too."

Somehow I just melted into his arms and buried my face in his shoulder. "It's so marvelous."

With a gentle squeeze he murmured, "Come on, chérie, let's go and have a long talk. There's so much to tell you, and probably not a lot of time."

As we walked back in the direction I'd just come from, he filled me in on final details of his flight and arrival, then described events of the previous weekend in Vienna.

"The magistrate to whom I stated my case freed me on a surprisingly small bond, because he said I was the first person he'd ever seen give himself up for dealing. Also because of the evidence I presented to him. But I'm getting ahead of myself. I'll back up."

"Yes, please do. *When* did you first know of the heroin on the coach, and *who* had it?"

"Hans, our coach driver, informed me Monday, the first night of the trip, about the H aboard, and of your danger. I nearly blew up, but I realized my hands were completely tied. As before, I couldn't go to the police because of my past. Once they got you, they could make me do whatever they asked. I wanted to kill Hans, Lord forgive me."

"Did he know about this before you all left Paris?"

"Just before; too late to do anything. At first, after he told me, he swore he didn't know who was carrying it. When I said that was impossible, he had to know, and that I'd expose him to the company immediately, he admitted having been bribed — but on pain of his life, he couldn't reveal the smuggler's identity. If we'd been in private — but he chose a very public place to tell me. Never mind where."

He'd shut his eyes, and I pictured a few possible places.

"I ran through the passenger list in my mind. The person, or persons, would most likely be traveling alone, I felt. We had several singles: there was a girl from India, in full garb — do you remember her? — who since then, incidentally, caused a nerve-wracking hassle at one border; a man from Turkey; an English lady; a couple more likely ones from Eastern Europe; and the rest

Americans — but no way to tell who, and he would not reveal it."

"Was it the Turk?"

"Interestingly, no, though I considered that possibility first. For both our sakes, I won't mention either names or nationalities, and there were two of them, both men. But as I told you on the phone, the whole mess was ghastly at the border checks, as I was now party to it; but mostly it was your danger that kept me in misery and constant turmoil — especially knowing about your trip to Marseille, even with Henri."

"If they'd known I was going and had traced my whereabouts in time, the Chateau d'If Island would certainly have been a perfect place to take me captive!"

"Only in fiction, ma chérie." A mere trace of humor crossed his face. "The night before we reached Vienna, I faced Hans with certain possibilities I won't burden you about. In short, I won him over. He's a happy Dutchman, caught in the middle and scared stiff, who only wants to keep out of trouble, and he believed I could keep it easy for him. I wished at the time that I had one tenth the confidence I talked him into!"

"Yes, I remember Hans," I said sadly, empathizing with him in such circumstances, in spite of the bribe he accepted, though with little choice.

"Anyhow, Hans had taken the responsibility for hiding the stuff in his private compartment; that is, the driver often shares it with me, but only he has the key. Strangely enough, it was to be delivered in Vienna. Melanie, the Lord was really in control, but I certainly didn't know it. Hans managed to pass me the stuff before the fellow was to get it from him, and I took it home — my only choice — and hid it. My nerves were so shot that my family said I looked terrible."

"Good grief, Ernst, talk about danger! What a chance you took!"

"Yes, we managed on the sly to hire another bus and driver for the evening sightseeing tour for the local guide to lead, then parked the coach at a police station before he gave the stuff to me. Then he spent the night in the station — with as little explanation as possible! Later I joined . . . well, I had no idea yet what I would do. I just hopped a taxi I'd called for and hoped I wasn't being tailed."

"Apparently you pulled off the coup successfully, thanks be to Him. Then after you got home, you called me in Marseille," I said, remembering his call at the Hardings'.

"Right, and was so relieved that you were safe, and totally unconscious of your danger, or mine. I wouldn't have told you for anything, though I almost said too much, for you could only worry helplessly."

"Or pray."

"I didn't believe in prayer then, or was disillusioned at least. A few hours later, how totally different!"

"Oh Ernst, I'm *so glad* it's all over!" I snuggled against his arms as we strolled hand in hand. "You knew who they were by then, of course?"

"Oh, yes, Hans had told me, and we made sure they were both occupied when we left the hotel with the coach for the police station. That *was* a coup." He chuckled as we approached one of Brussels' lovely little parks. "You know the rest, how I walked all over, thinking. . . ."

"You took a tremendous chance doing that."

"I didn't care. I had more important things to consider — more important than mere mortality." He looked deep into my eyes, and our spirits communed in complete understanding.

"Thank You, Lord Jesus," I murmured, and he nodded.

"You know, I found a verse in the Psalms yesterday, 49:20, that certainly describes my former state. It says, 'Man that is in honor, and understandeth not, is like the beasts that perish.' "

"Hm. True enough."

"So anyhow, first I prayed for His protection over my sleeping family and our home, for I knew they could easily find me or ransack the place. Since they hadn't found me by then, however, I figured they probably had split. I found later they had, but they didn't get far. Then I took the stuff and went directly back to the police station where Hans was, and presented the necessary evidence and as many names and whereabouts of the ring as I knew. Hans's part I played down as helpless victim. By then I was ready to drop from fatigue, so I slept there for two hours, then later that morning presented the whole thing to the magistrate. Also I had to explain some things to my company, who, as I told you, let me finish my tour. They've since relieved me of my next one, so the near future is still uncertain. Of course when the case comes to trial, I'll be at the mercy of the court."

"Have they caught all of the smuggling ring?"

"No, I don't think all of them. As I told you before, we never know everyone."

"Then we're still in danger!"

"Who cares, Melanie? We're in the Lord's hands, and hasn't He promised to protect us?"

"Yes, of course, or go with us through every trial. Nothing can separate us from His love in Christ."

"I found a verse, Monday or Tuesday, in II Timothy, chapter 4, 'The Lord shall deliver me from every evil work, and will preserve me unto His Heavenly Kingdom: to whom be glory for ever and ever.' You told me to claim promises and assurances in Scripture, and I've claimed it for myself. For you too."

"The very danger that drove you to Jesus Christ, your only help, no longer causes fear, for now you're secure in Him!"

"Yes." Once again that profound communion united our spirits.

"I have two more questions—Ilse and Henri. Where do they stand in all this?"

Sorrow, gratitude, and determination were by turn mirrored in his face. "I called Henri the other night, and he told me the whole bit. We owe Ilse, and Henri too, in part, for your safety and perhaps more. But I'm sure she's defecting. She used what she knew to try to protect us. I'm going to find her, Melanie, and tell her what the Lord has done for me. That's my second challenge, after my family. Henri wasn't involved in all this, except...," his jaw tightened, and regret filled his gaze, "I furnished him plenty of hash, and we used to smoke some. Never again. The desire is completely gone, Mel. A real miracle."

I nodded as I looked away, thinking of Henri and what we'd been through together, of his good heart in spite of all this.

"I told him what happened to me, and I'll have much more to say to him soon enough."

"Somehow I think you'll find him ready to listen, and maybe join us, Ernst. The Hardings and I have been praying for him."

"So have I." He bent his head and said in an anguished tone, "Oh Melanie, I have so much to make up for to so many, and especially to you."

I smiled gently, putting my hand on his. "There's *no condemnation*, not even guilt, bondage or self-judgment, to those who are in Christ Jesus, Ernst, dear."

"What comfort and assurance that is, darling." He squeezed my hand. "Now, please tell me all about Eurofest, and the schedule for today. I'm anxious to hear everything."

CHAPTER 22

We missed the skit at two o'clock, but Ernst registered, then we reached Heysel Stadium as the early crowds arrived, and made our way to the French section nearest the choir and speaker's rostrum to meet the others.

It wasn't long before I heard a familiar little voice, "There they are! Melanie!" Marg ran to me for a hug, then a shy, "Hi, Ernst."

He bent down and greeted her with, "Shalom, chère Marguerite Anne." She beamed in delight, and so did I.

Jim came to us, followed by Laurie and Aunt Kate. He and Ernst exchanged searching looks as they grasped hands.

"Welcome, Ernst," Jim said as he smiled broadly.

Eyes shining, Ernst answered, "Thank you, Jim, for your prayers and your ministry."

Jim reached his other arm around Ernst's shoulders, saying, "We're brothers in Christ now?"

I thought I detected a bit of mist in Ernst's eyes as he answered, "Yes, we sure are," and completed the half embrace.

Laurie reached out and shook Ernst's hand. "Welcome to His fellowship, Ernst. I'm so happy for you."

"Thank you for your part too, Madame. And this is?"

"Aunt Kate, Ernst Neubauer," I answered. "Katherine Daniels."

"How do you do, Ernst? Let me welcome you too," Aunt Kate said. "I've waited a long time for this, and the added joy of your new experience means more than I can say."

"Praise the Lord," he murmured, and our eyes met as the 250-voice choir began a warm-up practice on "How Great Thou Art" in Flemish, then in French.

"Here come the fellows from their explorations," Jim said as Johnny and David ascended the stands from an entrance below us. They both looked at Ernst, and Johnny grinned as he came up and greeted him.

"Hey, old friend. Good to see you again."

"Well, Johnny Alexander. I'm glad to see you back in Europe."

"Good to be back."

"Hi, David, are you having a good time?"

"Yes, sir. It sure is neat; glad you could come, too."

"So am I. This is *fantastisch,* especially for Belgium. I've never seen so many Bibles in one place in all my life."

Crowds were filling the stands even more than the night before, and the service soon began. Soloist and singing group were excellent, and the singing, led by Cliff Barrows, was magnificent. Thousands of us sang as one mighty voice the theme chorus of Eurofest:

> "He is Lord, He is Lord,
> He is risen from the dead and He is Lord.
> Every knee shall bow, every tongue confess
> That Jesus Christ is Lord."

Dr. Billy Graham preached a clear gospel sermon so all could understand God's plan of salvation.

"I offer you a living Christ who will come into your

hearts right now," he proclaimed. As he had so often before, he stated that he was going to ask all who wanted to receive Jesus Christ as Savior and Lord, to confess such a decision already made, or rededicate their lives to Him, to come down and stand on the track in front of their own language section to indicate their decision.

As the late afternoon sun sent its shining rays across the stadium, the choir joined by the rest of us began prayerfully singing in many different languages, but the same tune,

> "Just as I am, without one plea,
> But that Thy blood was shed for me,
> And that Thou bidd'st me come to Thee,
> Oh Lamb of God, I come."

Laurie and Jim quietly slipped out and started down as counselors. Ernst looked at me, smiled serenely, took my hand and murmured, "Let's go down, Melanie. I want to tell the world I'm a Christian now!"

Perfectly willing, my heart swelled with rejoicing as we stepped out hand in hand and descended to the track with the hundreds of others also coming to Christ.

We paused before our section among increasing numbers standing with bowed heads as the singing continued. I knew I'd remember these moments forever.

Jim saw us and came over with outstretched hand, saying softly, "God bless you both for coming. You'll never regret taking your stand here for Him. Remember John 5:24 ... You'll *never* come to judgment, for He took all your judgment on Himself on the cross. Be assured you *are* passed from death to eternal life no matter what happens or comes to you in the future." He put a hand on each of our shoulders and led us in a loving prayer of thanksgiving and assurance. "I'd better see to some of these others. God bless you both. See you afterward."

Laurie, who had been counseling a lady nearby, turned to us and said, "Your faces are so radiant, they're beautiful!"

We smiled at each other and thanked her, noticing radiant faces all around us, as well as tears. The music soon stopped, and crowds up in the stands began to disperse. Ernst looked across the field and suggested, "Let's go over there to the German section. Who knows....?"

Slowly we walked around the track among numerous groups of two or more reading God's Word aloud, speaking earnestly or praying together. Approaching the German section, we saw quite a number of couples or groups and noticed all had a counselor dealing with them and giving out literature, the same follow-up packets with Scripture portions that Jim had given us. The German I heard may as well have been Greek to my ears.

"See anyone you know?" I asked, and Ernst shook his head.

A few seconds later, one of the counselors finished with his companion, turned to us and spoke in German. I looked at Ernst, who answered him, his smile broadening as they carried on a short conversation. I saw by his ribbon badge that he was head counselor for the German section.

Then Ernst turned to me with a wide grin and said, "Melanie, here's one of your fellow Americans!"

I frowned in puzzlement as the fellow extended his hand to me with bright, sparkling eyes and a big smile, saying in English, "Larry Booker. I'm from the good ol' U.S.A., a missionary to Austria with Greater Europe Mission. Welcome to Eurofest. Your friend here told me about his recent decision for the Lord. You know Jesus as your Savior too?"

"I sure do, praise Him! Isn't this fantastic, Ernst?" I laughed in delight. "I'm from Richmond, Virginia. Ever been there?"

"Yes, I have. My family and I spent our first weekend there on our last furlough, visiting friends. I spoke, sang, and played my guitar in the Sunday School and at the youth meetings at their church, Immanuel Baptist."

"That's *my* church! Hallelujah! What a small world," I marveled, and Ernst nodded, eyes beaming.

"When Christians meet, it is often just that," Larry said.

We told him our names, and when he heard Ernst was from Vienna, he took down his address, as he lived about forty miles south of it in Mattersburg.

"It sure is good to meet you both. Hope we'll see you downtown at the music festival when I get all my reports in here. God bless you."

"Thank you, and you too. I'm sure we'll meet again," Ernst said as we parted.

"This is positively the most amazing and blessed experience I've ever had!" I exclaimed in pure joy as we again rounded the field back to the French section.

"My feelings exactly, to say the least," Ernst agreed.

"Ernst, look, there's Johnny, down here praying with Jim!"

Sure enough, Jim had his hand on my brother's shoulder, praying, and as we approached, we saw Laurie nod to us as she came over.

"Yes, Johnny came down too, a little while ago, to receive Jesus Christ as his Savior."

My eyes began to mist, and I cried, "Oh Father, You're so marvelous!" Ernst drew me to him, and we stood there as one, thanking our precious Lord.

In a few minutes they finished, and I went over and

hugged Johnny, now my brother not only by blood but in Christ.

After dinner we marveled at the endless lines of young people waiting to jam the special buses leaving for the Place Rogier downtown, joyfully singing gospel songs in all languages. We all, including Aunt Kate's friend, crowded into the Hardings' car, and somehow managed to find a parking place within about ten minutes' walk from the Place.

As we joined the crowds, Jim told us, "The Eurofest count is 7800 young people from 40 countries. Add to that thousands of others who will attend the Heysel meetings, and think of all here in Europe who will hear the gospel and respond, many for the first time!"

"Alleluia!" we heard thousands singing, and joined in as we approached the Place, jammed solid with people.

"It reminds me of Times Square on New Year's Eve," Laurie commented gaily.

"But what a difference in personnel," Jim said with a joyful smile.

It was a thrilling experience as the various soloists and musical groups presented a contemporary folk-type songfest par excellence with translation handled very effectively.

When it was over, Ernst and I said "So long" to the others, shoved through the mobs, and finally found a taxi back to my hotel.

"I left something at the desk today for your birthday, and I'd like for you to open it at our little park."

"Where we went today? How thoughtful you are."

At the hotel desk, the concierge handed him a small package, then we left, again strolling toward the park.

"What a superb day this has been, darling," I commented as we walked. "Think of all that's happened this summer to both of us. In spite of the bad things, how splendidly the Lord has worked!"

"Yes, 'to God be the glory, great things He hath done,' as that song we sang goes." He paused. "You deserve many thanks too, Melanie, for some of the things that helped bring me to Jesus."

"What in particular, Ernst?"

He chuckled thoughtfully. "Strangely enough, I believe the first thing that really got to me was that morning you came to my room, picked up my clothes and straightened the mess. After all, you'd pulled a complete switch on me, though you knew the arrangement. Frankly, I was finished with you. Frustrated, furious. What a fool!" He squeezed my shoulders to him. "Forgive me?"

"Long ago!" I smiled, remembering the prayers of my friends in Richmond although they had been prayed too late to prevent my first flare-up with Ernst.

"Then also, your consistent behavior — faithful to God's will as you knew it, in the face of . . ."

"Great temptation," I supplied. "Ernst, may I ask: Did you really mean it when you said you wouldn't touch me if I went with you on tour?"

Shame filled his countenance. "It's hard to be honest, but I confess I lied. I counted on your weakness. It was dishonorable from the first. I'm deeply sorry."

"There's *no* condemnation from Him or from me, chéri," I reminded him tenderly.

"That's it," he said quietly. "Of course, the most important part of all was your constant, patient love for me, even after you found out my past and present."

"I honestly love you."

As we reached the park, his arm still circling my shoulder, he bent his head and softly kissed my hair.

I thought, Why had I dared hope and pray for my love's

salvation? Was it not because I knew experientially, with every fiber of my being, that Jesus Christ is the only Way to the only true God . . . is absolute Truth . . . and is Life eternal? And as He did Ernst, does He not transform people?

"My family is very anxious to meet you, darling," he was saying. "After your course at the Alliance is finished, you're invited to Vienna to meet them."

"I'd love to, Ernst."

"They speak enough English to communicate all right," he teased.

"Hope so!"

We sat near the cascading fountain under bright stars in the little park, an island all ours.

"I found this little gift . . . many would say by chance, but I don't believe it . . . in a certain book shop. Blessed birthday, chérie."

Thanking him, I unwrapped my gift. It was a plaque on which was printed Psalm 34:3, and he read it aloud slowly: "O magnify the Lord with me, and let us exalt His name together." His eyes held mine. "In marriage, Melanie, together, forever?"

"Together, forever, yes," I answered, lifting my lips to his.